Business @ the Speed of Thought

BILL GATES

Level 6

Retold by Stephen Bryant
Edited by Mike Dean
Consultant Editor: David Evans
Series Editors: Andy Hopkins and Jocelyn Potter

Pearson Education Limited
Edinburgh Gate, Harlow,
Essex CM20 2JE, England
and Associated Companies throughout the world.

ISBN: 978-1-4058-8259-0

First published in the USA by Warner Books, a Time Warner Company 1999
New edition first published by Penguin Books Ltd 2001
This edition first published 2008

1 3 5 7 9 10 8 6 4 2

Typeset by Graphicraft Ltd, Hong Kong
Set in 11/14pt Bembo
Printed in China
SWTC/01

Published by Pearson Education Ltd in association with
Penguin Books Ltd, both companies being subsidiaries of Pearson Plc

For a complete list of the titles available in the Penguin Readers series please write to your local
Pearson Longman office or to: Penguin Readers Marketing Department, Pearson Education,
Edinburgh Gate, Harlow, Essex CM20 2JE, England.

Contents

Introduction

"As the boss of Microsoft, the world's most successful software company, I played a large part in the birth of the Information Age. In this book I explain the idea of a digital nervous system—the use of information technology to satisfy people's needs at work and at home . . ."

In 1980, IBM was the world's biggest producer of business machines, but the world was changing. Small computers were beginning to appear and the company wanted to get into that market. They began to develop a machine which they called the Personal Computer, but it needed an operating system.

At the time they were talking to Microsoft, a small company that sold computer programs, and they happened to mention the problem. Microsoft didn't have an operating system, but they knew someone who did. They bought the rights to it and after making changes to suit the new PC, sold it to IBM as MS-DOS. However, Bill Gates, the boss of Microsoft, insisted that IBM should allow him to keep the rights to the system, so that he could also sell it to other customers. Surprisingly, IBM agreed.

Gates had correctly realized that a computer was simply a box to run the software. The IBM PC appeared in 1981, but other manufacturers moved in and started selling similar machines. Most of them used MS-DOS. Within a few years Microsoft changed from being a small software company to a very large one. Meanwhile, IBM never managed to dominate the personal computer market and finally stopped making these machines in 2005.

Today, there are large companies such as Dell, Hewlett-Packard and Toshiba selling personal computers. However, there are also huge numbers of "white-box" machines—built from standard parts by small companies, stores, or interested people. Most of them use Microsoft software.

In 1985, Microsoft introduced its Windows program. Before this, computer screens were plain and files simply appeared as lines of text. Windows made the screen colorful and more user-friendly. It also allowed the operator to do more tasks more easily and made better use of the computer's memory. Five years later, Microsoft Office appeared. This contained Microsoft Word for writing texts, Excel for calculations, and Powerpoint, which allowed the user to give presentations.

Microsoft's biggest crisis, which Bill Gates discusses in this book, came in August 1995, when the company, having underestimated how quickly the Internet was growing in popularity, released Windows 95 without Internet Explorer. However, they very quickly produced an improved version.

Today Microsoft has 79,000 employees in 102 countries. Its annual earnings are over $50 billion. At times, its most popular products—the various versions of Microsoft Windows and Office—have taken more than 90% of the market. Recently, however, there are signs that the company, like IBM before it, may be slowing down. Free software, available on the Internet, has taken away a large share of new sales, and the MSN search engine comes third after Google and Yahoo. However, new products are promised.

Bill Gates was born in October 28, 1955, in Seattle, where he grew up with his two sisters and where he still lives with his wife and children. He became interested in programming while he was at school and at the age of fourteen, with Paul Allen, another Lakeside student, he formed a company called Traf-O-Data, to make traffic counters. In the first year he earned $20,000. In 1973 he went to Harvard to study math. There he met Steve Ballmer, now president of Microsoft.

In January 1975 the magazine *Popular Electronics* offered a very simple computer, the Altair 8800, for hobbyists. Programming it was a slow process which involved setting many switches, but Bill Gates contacted MITS, the manufacturer of the Altair, to say that he and others were working on a version of BASIC that would run on it. MITS was interested and the result was Altair Basic. It used a long piece of paper with holes in it. The first question typed in was 2+2, and the machine said 4. This was the beginning of personal computers. Gates left Harvard soon afterwards and started Microsoft with Paul Allen.

In 1995 Bill Gates wrote *The Road Ahead*, which was number one in the New York Times best-seller list for seven weeks and is also a Penguin Reader. *Business @ the Speed of Thought* came out in 1999. In it, Bill Gates compares the Internet to the human nervous system. We sense what is happening around us, messages are sent to the brain, and it tells the body what to do. Gates offers this model as the way a company should behave, with websites and e-mail allowing it minute-by-minute contact with its customers and changes in the market, while inside the company, data and ideas can move quickly between employees and managers.

The result can be a better future as more and better information provides more interesting jobs for workers, more knowledgeable customers, more effective schools, and citizens who have a voice in the decisions of their governments. A "digital nervous system" can improve business—but this book is not only for people in business, it is for everyone.

Chapter 1   Information Flow is Your Lifeblood

Information work is thinking work. When thinking and working together are significantly assisted by computer technology, you have a digital nervous system. It consists of the advanced digital processes that knowledge workers use to make better decisions —to think, act, react, and adapt. Michael Dertouzos of MIT writes that the future " Information Marketplace " will require a large amount of special software and complex combinations of human and machine processes—an excellent description of a digital nervous system at work.

Do you view information technology as a way to solve specific problems? Then you're probably only getting a fraction of the benefits that modern computers and software can provide. Instead, you should be creating systems that will deliver information immediately to anyone who can use it—" digital nervous systems."

As the boss of Microsoft, the world's most successful software company, I played a large part in the birth of the Information Age. In this book I explain the idea of a digital nervous system— the use of information technology to satisfy people's needs at work and at home, just as the human nervous system supports the human mind.

Like a living creature, an organization works best if it can rely on a nervous system that sends information immediately to the parts that need it. A digital nervous system can unite all of an organization's systems and processes, releasing rivers of information and allowing businesses to make huge leaps in efficiency, growth, and profits. I have a simple but strong belief: how you gather, manage, and use information will decide whether you win or lose.

1

The best way to put distance between your company and the crowd is to do an excellent job with information. There are more competitors today. There is more information available about them and about the market, which is now worldwide. The winners will be the ones who develop a world-class digital nervous system so that information can easily flow through their companies for maximum and constant learning.

I know what you're going to say: no, it's efficient processes! It's quality! It's winning market share and creating brands that are recognized! It's getting close to customers! Success, of course, depends on all of these things. Nobody can help you if your processes aren't efficient, if you don't care about quality, if you don't work hard to build your brand, if your customer service is poor. A bad business plan will fail however good your information is. And bad practice will spoil a good plan. If you do enough things badly, you'll go out of business.

But whatever else you have on your side today—smart employees, excellent products, loyal customers, cash in the bank —you need a fast flow of good information to make processes efficient, raise quality, and improve the way you put your plan into practice. Most companies have good people working for them. Most companies want to treat their customers well. Good, useful data exists somewhere within most organizations. Information flow is the lifeblood of your company because it enables you to get the most out of your people and to learn from your customers. See if you have the information to answer these questions:

- What do customers think about your products? What problems do they want you to fix? What new features do they want you to add?

- What problems do your partners have as they sell your products or work with you?
- Where are your competitors winning business from you, and why?
- Will customers' changing demands force you to develop new capacities?
- What new markets are appearing that you should enter?

A digital nervous system won't guarantee you the right answers to these questions. But it will free you from the old paper processes so that you'll have the time to think about the questions. It will give you the data to start thinking immediately, and to see the trends coming at you. A digital nervous system will make it possible for facts and ideas to quickly surface from deep in your organization, from the people who have information about these questions and, it's likely, many of the answers. Most important, it will allow you to do all these things fast.

◆

An old business joke says that if the railroads had understood that they were in the transport business instead of the steel-rail business, we'd all be flying on Union Pacific Airlines. Many businesses have changed their goals in even more basic ways. But it's not always clear where the next growth opportunity is.

McDonald's has the strongest brand name and market share and a good reputation for quality. But a market analysis recently suggested the company change its business model. McDonald's has occasionally promoted movie-linked toys. The analysis suggested that the company should use its well-known small-profit product to sell the high-profit toys, and not the other way round. Such a change is unlikely, but not unthinkable in today's fast-changing business world.

3

No company can assume that its position in the market is safe. A company should constantly be thinking about its options. One company might be hugely successful if it broke into another business. Another company might find that it should stay with what it knows and does best. The most important thing is that a company's managers have the information to understand where they can compete and what their next great market could be.

This book will help you to use information technology to ask and answer the hard questions about what your business should be and where it should go. Information technology gives you the data that leads to deeper understanding of your business. It enables you to act quickly. It provides solutions to business problems that simply weren't available before. Information technology and business are becoming so tightly linked that you can't talk about one without talking about the other.

◆

The first step in answering any hard business question is to look at the facts. It's easier to say this than to do it. The principle is illustrated in my favorite business book, *My Years with General Motors*, by Alfred P. Sloan Jr. If you only read one business book, read Sloan's (but don't put this one down to do it). Extraordinary success can follow from positive leadership that's based on information and reason.

During Sloan's time as boss, from 1923 to 1956, General Motors became one of the first really complex business organizations in the United States. Sloan understood that a company could not develop a broad business plan or choose the right projects without building on facts and on the understanding of the people in the company. He developed his own understanding of the business by working closely with his staff and by regular personal visits to the company's technical departments. His greatest influence as a manager, however, came from creating working relationships with GM dealers across the country. He constantly gathered information from GM's dealers, and he worked to develop close relationships with them that produced results.

Sloan thought that fact-finding trips were very important. So he built an office in a private railroad car and traveled all over the country, visiting dealers. He often saw between five and ten dealers a day. These visits helped Sloan to see that the car business was changing. It was moving from simple selling to trading, as people wanted to trade their old cars when they bought new ones. Sloan saw that GM's relationship with its dealers had to change as well. The manufacturer and the dealers had to become partners. Sloan formed a dealer council to meet regularly with GM's senior executives. He also created a department to handle complaints from the dealers. He paid for economic studies to find the best places for new dealers, and even found a way to lend money to "capable men" who did not have the cash to become dealers.

Accurate information about sales was still hard to find. When a dealer's profits went down, GM didn't know why. Without the facts, it was impossible to know what to do. Sloan said he would pay a lot of money so that every dealer "could know the facts about his business and could intelligently deal with the many details ... in an intelligent manner." This would be "the best investment General Motors ever made."

Sloan created a standardized system of accounts for the entire GM organization and all its dealers. Every dealer and every employee, at every level of the company, put their numbers into exactly the same categories. By the mid-1930s GM's dealers, its factories, and its offices could all do detailed financial analysis using the same numbers. A dealer, for example, could clearly see how well he was doing and also compare his results to the average across the company.

An infrastructure that provided accurate information led to a company that responded quickly to events. Other car makers could not compete with GM for decades. This infrastructure—what I call a company's nervous system—helped GM to dominate the car business throughout Sloan's career. It wasn't yet digital, but it was extremely valuable.

Of course, you couldn't get nearly as much information flowing through your company then as you can now. It would have required too many phone calls and too many people moving paper around and looking at the data to find patterns. It would have been very expensive. If you want to run a world-class company today, you have to obtain much more data and do it much faster. To manage with the force of facts—one of Sloan's business principles—requires information technology.

If information management and quick responses made such a basic difference in a traditional industry seventy years ago, how much more difference will they make when they are powered by information technology? A modern car maker may have a strong brand name and a reputation for quality today but it is facing even greater competition from around the world.

All car makers use the same steel and the same machines; they have similar manufacturing processes and they have roughly the same transport costs. Today the tests of success are how well they design their products, how intelligently they use information from their customers to improve their products and services, how quickly they can improve their production processes, how cleverly they market their products, and how efficiently they deliver their products and services to customers. All of these processes are rich in information and they benefit from digital technology.

◆

The value of a digital approach is especially clear in businesses such as banks and insurance companies where information is central to the business. In banking, data about customers is the heart of the business, and banks have always been big users of information technology. Crestar Bank of Richmond, Virginia, offers all its banking services over the Internet. It has bank employees in supermarkets and malls who can offer banking services to customers using digital information flow.

In the age of the Internet and increasing competition in financial markets, the key to success is the intelligence of a bank's use of data and how well it responds to its customers. It's brains that give one bank or another the advantage. But I don't just mean the individual abilities of bank employees. I mean the overall ability of the bank to make use of the best thinking of all its employees.

After the introduction of ENIAC, the first general-purpose computer, during the Second World War, computers quickly proved that they were faster and more accurate than humans at many tasks. Computers were not working at a high level, though. They assisted people but not in an intelligent way. It takes brains to understand the physics of a rocket; it takes a computer to do the sums in seconds.

◆

Businesses need to do another kind of work, "information work." This phrase comes from Michael Dertouzos, director of MIT's laboratory for computer science, and author of *What Will Be*. We usually think of information—a letter, a picture, or a financial report—as something that doesn't change. But Dertouzos argues that another form of information is active. Information work is the processing of information by human brains or computer programs.

Information work—designing a building, making a deal, filling in tax forms—is most of the work done in developed countries. Dertouzos estimates that information work contributes 50 to 60 percent of the total value of the goods and services produced by an industrialized country.

Dertouzos's idea is important. When computers went from simple number-work to modeling business problems, they began to play a part in information work. Even manufacturing firms have always put more energy into information about the work than into the work itself: information about product design and development; about marketing, sales, and supplies; about payments and finance; about cooperating with sellers; about customer service.

To do information work, people in the company have to be able to find information easily. Until recently though, we've been told that "the numbers" should be reserved for the most senior executives. Sometimes there are good reasons for secrecy, but usually information has been reserved simply because it took time, money, and effort to move information around, so you had to be senior to order the work. On today's computer networks you can find and present data easily and cheaply. You can dive into the data to the lowest level of detail and look at it from different angles. You can exchange information and ideas with other people. You can bring together the ideas and work of many people for a better result.

We need to stop thinking that getting information and moving information around is difficult and expensive. It's just basic common sense to make all of your company's data easily available to every person who can use it.

All of a company's employees, not just its high-level executives, need to see business data. It's important for me as a Chief Executive Officer, (CEO), to understand how the company is doing across regions or product lines or different types of customer, and I take pride in staying informed. However, it's the middle managers in every company who need to understand where their profits and losses come from, what marketing programs are working or not, and what expenses are under control or too high. They're the people who need accurate, useful data because they're the ones who need to act. They shouldn't have to wait for upper management to bring information to them. Companies should spend less time protecting financial data from employees and more time teaching them to analyze and act on it.

In many companies the middle managers can drown in day-to-day problems and not have the information they need to fix them. A sign of a good digital nervous system is that middle managers are made more effective by the flow of accurate, useful information. The systems should tell them about unusual events—for example, if an expense item is too high. Then the managers don't need to look at normal expense activity. Some companies work like this, but I'm constantly surprised by how few companies use information technology to keep their middle managers well-informed and avoid routine review.

I'm amazed by the twisted path that important information often takes through many Fortune 500 companies. At McDonald's, until recently, sales data had to be "touched" by hand several times before it made its way to the people who needed it. Today McDonald's is installing a new information system that processes sales at all of its restaurants in real time. As soon as you order two Happy Meals, a McDonald's marketing manager will know. So that manager will have hard facts to analyze sales, not unreliable data.

As we'll see in the description of Microsoft's reaction to the Internet, another sign of a good digital nervous system is the number of good ideas coming from your middle managers and knowledge workers. When they can analyze real data, people get detailed ideas about how to do things better—and they get excited, too. People like knowing that something they're doing is working and they like being able to show managers that it's working. They enjoy using technology that encourages them to test different theories about what's happening in their markets. People really appreciate information.

A final sign of a good digital nervous system is how effective your face-to-face meetings are. Good meetings are the result of good preparation. Meetings shouldn't be used mainly to present information. It's more efficient to use e-mail* so that people can analyze data before the meeting. Then they will be prepared to make suggestions and debate the issues at the meeting itself.

Companies that are struggling with too many unproductive meetings don't lack energy and brains. The data they need exists somewhere in the company in some form. Digital tools would enable them to get the data immediately, from many sources, and to analyze it from many angles.

GM's Alfred Sloan said that without facts it's impossible to put an effective plan into action. I believe that if you have good facts, you can put an effective plan into action. Sloan did, many times over. At the speed business moves today, we need more than ever to manage with the force of facts.

What I'm describing here is a new level of information analysis that enables knowledge workers to turn raw data into active information—what Michael Dertouzos calls knowledge-as-a-verb. A digital nervous system enables a company to do information work with more efficiency, depth, and creativity.

Can your digital nervous system do this?

Like a human being, a company needs an internal communication system, a "nervous system," to organize its actions. All businesses concentrate on a few basic things: customers, products and services, earnings, costs, competitors, delivery, and employees. A company has to carry out the business processes in each area and

*e-mail: electronic mail.

make sure that they are working together, especially activities that cross departments.

The sales department needs to find out quickly whether the company can supply a product before promising to deliver a big order. The manufacturing department needs to know what product is selling strongly so that it can change production priorities. Business managers throughout the company need to know about both—and a lot more, too.

An organization's nervous system has parallels with our human nervous system. Every business has some processes that must continue for the company to survive, just as the human heart must keep beating. The need to be efficient and reliable has driven companies to automate many of these basic operations. But because managers have taken whatever solution was available, the result over time has been a large number of systems that don't always work together. Each independent system may work smoothly on its own, but the data in each is isolated and difficult to combine with the data in the others. Getting data about operational processes and using it has been one of the more difficult problems of business. But today's technology can make basic operations the basis of a much broader, company-wide intelligence.

A company needs to respond quickly and well to any crisis or unplanned event. You might get a call from your best customer saying he's buying from your biggest competitor, or that competitor might introduce a great new product, or you might have a faulty product or an operation that breaks down. Unplanned events can be positive, too. You might get an unexpected opportunity for a major new activity or purchase.

Finally, there's the conscious directing of your company's muscles, whether you're creating teams to develop new products, opening new offices, or sending people out to win new customers. To be carried out well, these planned events need careful thinking and strategic analysis before and after you act.

You need to think about your company's basic business issues, and develop a long-term business plan to solve problems and take advantage of the opportunities your analysis reveals. Then you need to communicate what you want to do, and the plans behind it, to every person in the company and to partners and other relevant people outside the company.

More than anything, though, a company has to communicate with its customers and act on what it learns from them. This primary need involves all of a company's capacities: operational efficiency, data gathering, cooperation, strategic planning, and action. The need to communicate with your customers will be emphasized again and again in this book. I'll show how a digital nervous system helps successful companies to do this.

A digital nervous system serves two primary purposes in developing business understanding. It extends the individual's capacity for analysis the way machines extend physical capacities, and it combines the abilities of individuals to create a company intelligence and act as one. To put it all together: A digital nervous system seeks to create company excellence out of individual excellence to serve the customer.

◆

A digital nervous system gives the people working for your company the same kind of data for daily business use that you give to someone you bring in to consult them about a problem. With their years of experience in the industry and their knowledge of business analysis, consultants often come in with new ideas after they have gone through the data. But isn't it crazy that someone outside the company receives more information than you use for yourself? Too often important customer and sales information is pulled together only when a consultant arrives. You should have that information there every day ready to be used by your employees. Your managers should have information of the same quality that the consultant has. As we'll see in the following example, good things happen when they have that information.

At Microsoft, our sales team calls only on large corporations. So every year Jeff Raikes, the man in charge of sales and support, struggles with the problem of how to market to small and medium-sized customers. We usually reach these customers through seminars and marketing with partners. But where are most of these customers? Are they all in the largest cities? Which cities should we choose for marketing?

From the Internet, we found the average number of employees per company per city. From outside consultants we got information on the number of personal computers (PCs) per city. From our marketing managers we got information on our seminars and our work with partners. Finally, we included the number of partners per city.

Using computers, we looked for a match between sales numbers and marketing activity. A Microsoft software program, MS Sales, gave us data in two important areas: last year's sales data, which helped us calculate growth, and income from sales by postal area. We found eighty cities that we thought were likely candidates for a new marketing campaign. But at Microsoft, before we invest money we want to know if the idea will work. We checked the eighty cities again using a marketing program, looking for an eight to one return on investment (ROI). Setting the ROI as high as eight to one would help us take out any cities where the percentage return might be high, but the absolute dollar return would be low. This gave us forty-five cities, later reduced to thirty-eight.

In each of those thirty-eight cities in which we hadn't done any marketing before, we held two "Big Day" events. On each Big Day we showed Microsoft products and made sales offers, with our partners. The ROI was an amazing twenty to one—$30 million return on $1.5 million investment. As the Big Day events happened, we used the MS Sales program to measure our return against figures in similar markets to see if the Big Days were really making a difference. The results: cities in which we did Big Day events showed a 57 percent increase in income against a 16 percent increase in income in a control group of nineteen small cities that did not have Big Days.

Today the program which identified the target cities has been improved, so that anybody in the company can see future sales opportunities not just by area, but by product, too. So instead of a seminar with all Microsoft products, we can find out if one city needs a seminar on Microsoft Office, another on Windows, and a third on Exchange.

All that was because of the MS Sales program. A paper system could not do that work. The sales data now comes to us in a way that lets us put it into MS Sales immediately. This is inexpensive, and because we share this data with our partners, discussions with them about future marketing plans achieve better results. These discussions are still old fashioned face-to-face meetings, but everybody at those meetings is better prepared because of the data they have seen in advance.

At Microsoft our information systems have also changed the role of our managers. When MS Sales first came online, one of our managers in Minneapolis checked sales in her area at a level of detail not possible before. She discovered that the excellent total sales figures for her district hid poor sales to large customers. Finding that out came as a shock to the large customer sales team, but it was also the first step toward putting things right. By the end of the year Minneapolis was the fastest growing area for sales to large customers.

If you're a manager at Microsoft today, you must be more than a good sales team leader. Now you can be a business thinker because you have the data to help you run your business. You can look at sales figures and see where your business is strong and where it is weak, and which products you can sell, in which areas, to which size firms. You can try out new programs and look at the results. You can talk to other managers about what they're doing to get good results. Managers at Microsoft have a much more important role now than they did five years ago because of the easy-to-use computer programs that we've developed.

◆

A digital nervous system gives its users an understanding and an ability to learn things that they would not otherwise have. A good flow of information and good tools for analysis let us see new opportunities for profit among large amounts of data. It makes the best use of the capacities of human brains and reduces human labor.

To begin creating a digital nervous system, you should first develop an ideal picture of the information you need to run your business and to understand your markets and your competitors. Think hard about the facts you need to know. Develop a list of the most important questions for your business. Then demand that your information systems provide the answers. If your current system won't do this, you need to develop one that will. If you don't, one or more of your competitors will.

You know you have built an excellent digital nervous system when information flows through your organization as quickly and naturally as thought in a human being, and when you can use technology to organize teams of people as quickly as you can direct an individual. It's business at the speed of thought.

Digital technology can completely change your production processes and your business processes. It can also free workers from slow paper processes. Replacing paper processes with digital processes frees knowledge workers to do more useful work. The all-digital work place is usually called "the paperless office," a phrase that goes back to at least 1973. It's a great vision. No more piles of paper in which you can't find what you need. No more searching through heaps of reports to find marketing information or a sales number. But the paperless office never seems to actually arrive.

The Xerox Corporation did more to promote the concept than any other company. In 1974-5 it was talking about the "office of the future" that would have computers and e-mail with information online. Between 1975 and 1987 several business newspapers promised that the paperless office wasn't far off but in 1988 I told a journalist, "This vision of a paperless office is still very, very far away."

Today we have all the pieces in place to achieve the paperless office. Better computers and software make it easy to combine data of various types. Highly capable, networked PCs are everywhere in the office environment. The Internet is connecting PCs around the world. But paper use has continued to double every four years, and 95 percent of all information in the United States remains on paper, compared with just 1 percent stored electronically. Paper is increasing faster than digital technology can reduce it!

In 1996 I decided to look at ways that Microsoft was still using paper. To my surprise, we had printed 350,000 paper copies of sales reports that year. I asked for a copy of every paper form we used. The thick file that landed on my desk contained hundreds and hundreds of forms. Paper use was only a sign of a bigger problem, though: administrative processes that were too complicated and took too much time.

I looked at the file and wondered, "Why do we have all these forms? Every person here has a PC. We're connected up. Why aren't we using electronic forms and e-mail?" As Chief Executive Officer I gave the order to ban all unnecessary forms. In place of all that paper, systems grew up that were more accurate and easier to work with and that freed our people to do more interesting work.

Now, even before we employ a new worker, he or she starts on an electronic journey. We receive career information from 600 to 900 people applying for jobs every day, through the post, by e-mail at resume@microsoft.com, or at the Microsoft website at www.microsoft.com/jobs. Seventy percent of the career information now arrives by e-mail or to the website, up from 6 percent two years ago and rising. All career information from people applying for jobs is matched with open jobs within forty-eight hours, sometimes within twenty-four hours.

A software program sets up job interviews. Every interviewer gets career details of the person applying for the job by e-mail. After the interview each interviewer sends comments on the candidate by e-mail. This sharing of information makes sure that interviewers build on each other's work, not repeat it. If it is obvious that Microsoft wants the candidate, an e-mail signal tells the interviewer to explain to that person why Microsoft would be a good choice for them.

Let's say that someone called Sharon Holloway accepts our job offer. The imaginary Sharon is one of the eighty-five new people we employ each week. We'll say that Sharon is at Redmond, Washington. Before Sharon arrives at Microsoft, an administration assistant in her new department fills out the New Hire form on Microsoft's intranet* to request office furniture, and a computer

*intranet: a network of computers linked within a company.

with software, e-mail, and voice mail to be ready for Sharon. The same form makes sure that Sharon's name is added to the company phone list and that she gets a nameplate for her office door and a mailbox in the building's mailroom.

When she arrives, Sharon goes online to read the employee handbook (it doesn't exist on paper now) and she downloads any software she needs. Next, Sharon uses a program called MS Market to order office supplies, books, a whiteboard, and business cards. MS Market automatically puts in her name, her e-mail address, and the name of her manager on the order. The suppliers receive her request by e-mail and deliver the supplies to her office. An order above a certain amount of money would automatically go to a manager before it went to the supplier.

Sharon's paycheck goes into her account by e-mail and if she wants to she can change her bank online. For travel, Sharon uses a program designed by Microsoft in partnership with American Express, called AXI. It's available online twenty-four hours a day, seven days a week.

Some people think that "Microsofties" have no life outside the company, but actually they do. Sharon gets married and goes on vacation with her new husband. She enters her vacation time online. When she and her husband move into a new house, Sharon enters her new address online once and it is automatically sent to every department that needs her address. She visits our intranet to get information about bus routes and ride sharing in her new neighborhood.

When Sharon and her husband have a baby, she goes online to learn about seminars for parents, paid time off work for parents, and day care for children. Microsoft pays a certain amount in benefits to every person the company employs and they can take these benefits in many ways. They can look at different ways of combining benefits online. She can also buy and sell shares online, using the company that buys and sells shares for everybody

18

employed at Microsoft, Saloman Smith Barney. Sharon can buy and sell shares in Microsoft and use her vote as a shareholder online.

Using our computer network to replace paper forms has produced impressive results for us. As I write this book, we have reduced the number of paper forms from more than 1,000 to a company-wide total of sixty forms. Overall, the savings from using electronic forms have amounted to at least $40 million in our first twelve months of use in 1997–8. The biggest savings came from the reduction in processing costs. Accounting firms put the cost of each paper order—mostly the time of all the people handling the paper—at about $145. Electronic processing at Microsoft costs less than $5 per order.

As we invented new solutions, our central information-technology budget, which covers these and other major business areas, decreased 3 percent between 1996 and 1999, mostly from standardizing data and reducing the number of information systems we have.

Electronic tools give us benefits beyond reducing costs. For example, our Microsoft Market software asks for authority before it will process a request. This prevents the inappropriate purchases that can easily get through a paper-based system. Delivery information is typed instead of handwritten, so almost nothing is ever sent to the wrong destination. Communication with our suppliers is documented, and we know the costs in advance so there are no surprises. Our suppliers get paid faster, which means they want to deliver quickly. We're always discovering new benefits.

The move from paper to electronic forms is an essential step in developing a modern organization's nervous system, but you should use the change to improve processes that are central to your business. A digital nervous system is easy to build on. A good network, a good e-mail system, and easy-to-build webpages are everything you need for getting rid of internal paper forms, too. Our internal tools have two goals: to use software to handle routine tasks, so that our knowledge workers don't waste time and energy; and to free people to do more difficult work and handle unusual situations. Our internal developers use the "soft-boiled egg" rule: A user must be able to get into and out of most administrative tools within three minutes. This makes sure that we don't create clumsy tools and cause more work overall.

Improving administrative and internal business processes is an important way to improve the overall efficiency of your employees. When you give knowledge workers good internal tools, you also send them an important message: when employees see a company improve efficiency and get rid of time-draining routine administrative tasks, they know that the company values their time and wants them to use it profitably.

It's easy to measure when you make your factory workers more efficient. It's hard to measure when you make your knowledge workers more effective, but it makes sense that workers who aren't burdened by routine tasks will do better work. The benefit to customers is that your employees spend less time on paperwork and more time on customer needs.

Chapter 2   Commerce: The Internet Changes Everything

Ride the rocket of change

Not long ago I gave a talk to the board of directors of a German financial institution. These were experienced businesspeople. The youngest person there was probably fifty-five, and many of them were in their sixties. They'd seen a lot of changes in banking and they'd lived through a lot of technology changes, too. The bank had not yet, though, begun to use the new Internet technologies.

On the day of my visit they'd heard a series of talks from Microsoft employees about the company. When I walked into the room, they were all sitting there with their arms folded across their chests, looking unhappy.

"OK," I said. "What's the problem?"

One of them replied, "We think that banking is in the process of changing completely, and we're getting technical talks from people here at Microsoft—more technical than we're used to." He took his glasses off and rubbed his eyes and said, "This is probably good, although it's making us tired." After a pause he continued. "It's good that you're just going to make all of your products better, but what is the overall plan? To view you as a long-term supplier, we need you to give us a vision of the future. What are your organizing principles for development?"

The senior Microsoft executive who ends a meeting with customers doesn't usually bring a prepared talk. Instead, the person answers questions and makes a summary of what we'll do in response to any important issues that have come up. So as I stood in front of the German bankers I was thinking, "Oh boy. We've spent eight hours talking to this bank and we haven't answered the customer's central concerns. Now I've got to do it without notes . . ."

But by that time I'd given my talk on the digital nervous system a couple of dozen times, and I'd been working on this book for almost a year. So I began to write down the major changes that I thought were going to happen with technology in the near future. I was writing down ten changes that I thought would have a significant effect on industries, I told the bankers. These were important changes in customer behavior that were all related to digital technology and were all happening now.

"I'm going to ask you whether you believe each of them will happen. Don't worry now about how quickly, just tell me whether you believe they're ever going to occur. If you don't believe they will, then you shouldn't change what you're doing with technology. But if you believe they're going to happen, and it's only a matter of time, then you should start to prepare for that change today."

"Do you believe that in the future people at work will use computers every day for most of their jobs?" I asked. "Today a lot of people use computers occasionally, but many knowledge workers may use their PCs only a few times a day. They may even go a couple of days without using PCs. Do you believe that today's paperwork will be replaced by more efficient digital processes?" They did.

"Do you believe that one day most homes will have computers? In the United States today, about half of all homes have PCs. The percentage is a bit higher in some countries but much lower in most others. Do you believe," I asked, "that one day computers will be as common in homes as telephones or TVs?" They did.

"Do you believe that one day most businesses and most homes will have high-speed connections to the World Wide Web?" I asked. They nodded agreement.

"Do you believe e-mail will become as common a method of communication among people in business and homes as the telephone or paper mail is today? Today not everybody uses e-mail even if they have a computer. Will that situation change?" They agreed that it would.

"Now, if most people have computers and use them every day," I asked, "do you believe that most information will start arriving in digital form? Do you think your bills will arrive electronically? Do you think you'll be booking your travel arrangements over the Internet?" They agreed that these changes were coming.

"Do you think digital equipment will become common?" I asked. "Do you think that all phones, cameras, videos, and TVs will soon be digital? Do you think that other new machines will appear in the home and be connected to the Web?" It was only a matter of time, they agreed.

"Do you see a time coming when notebook computers become computer notebooks?" I described what I meant: a computer notebook is a new machine that enables you to take notes as you do today on paper and lets you carry with you all the personal and professional data you need. This will probably be the last change to occur. "The great thing about a computer notebook," I said, "is that however much you put into it, it doesn't get bigger or heavier." They laughed. There was a thirty-second conversation in German before one of them said, "We thought you said something funny, and then we realized you said something important."

"Am I wasting your time?" I asked. "Do you believe these changes are ever going to happen?" By now we were beginning to have a conversation. They had a short talk among themselves in German. The banker who had spoken before said, "We've been talking about the same things at home and, yes, we believe it's going to happen. When it does, it's going to completely change the nature of banking."

"When do you think it is going to happen?" I asked. They had another, longer conversation in German. Then they said, "We didn't expect to make this decision here, but we have. We were going to tell you twenty years, but then we decided that within ten years these changes will either have arrived or be coming very soon. Banking will be completely different."

"To prepare for that change," I told them, "you need to make digital information flow everywhere in your organization." I talked briefly about the need to use the digital tools that they already had for their knowledge workers. I talked about digitally linking their knowledge systems with business information systems to create a new infrastructure around the PC and Internet technologies. If they did these things, I told them, they would be prepared for the three basic business changes that will occur as the result of all the technological advances:

1. Most of the contact between business and customers, business and business, and people and government will become digital and self-service.

2. Customer service will become the primary way of adding value in every business. Human involvement in service will shift from routine, low-value tasks to high-value personal service to the customer.

3. The speed of digital operations and the need for more personal attention to customers will encourage companies to adopt digital processes internally if they have not yet adopted them for efficiency reasons. Companies will use a digital nervous system to regularly adapt their internal business processes to an environment that constantly changes because of customer needs and competition.

Complex customer-service and business problems would require powerful computers on both sides of the relationship— customer and employee—I said. The new relationships would be helped by various electronic aids such as voice, video, and interactive use of the same computer screen. We'd see a world in which fairly simple personal-companion computers became common alongside extremely powerful general-purpose PCs that support knowledge work at home or the office.

"Microsoft's vision," I ended by saying, "is to provide software that links all these digital machines together and enables people to create digital solutions based on the Web lifestyle. It's as simple as that."

The German bank board had a final question for me, which is the question on everyone's mind: what should they do personally to get ready for this new digital world? My answer was: use the tools yourselves. Senior executives should use e-mail and other electronic tools to get familiar with the new way of doing things.

They should see what their competitors' Internet sites look like. They should become Internet users. Buy some books and arrange some travel over the Internet, I told them, and see what it's like. If you're going to lead the digital age, you need to become familiar enough with the Internet to be able to imagine what the Web lifestyle will mean for your industry—even if the change is going to take years.

◆

For years and years enthusiasts have been saying that the Internet will happen "tomorrow." You're going to keep reading predictions that the big change will happen in the next twelve months. This is just garbage. The social changes that have to occur take years, and the infrastructure has to be extended. But when the social and technical changes reach a certain point, the change will be quick and permanent. The point will come where the Web lifestyle really will take off, and I believe that's some time in the next five years. As I said in *The Road Ahead*, we always overestimate the change that will occur in the next two years and underestimate the change that will occur in the next ten. Don't let yourself be fooled into doing nothing.

It's hard to think of a business category in which the Internet won't have an effect or in which there aren't already new Internet companies. Lots of firms now wish they were the first Internet book store or travel agency, winning the first customers, the public enthusiasm, the famous name.

Internet companies are not just learning new ways to do business. They are also rushing to break down the barriers between different areas of business. Amazon.com, which began as an Internet bookseller, has begun to sell CDs. There's no reason for Amazon not to sell other products as well. The initial reason for your company to go onto the Web might be to obtain cost savings and attract new customers. When you have customers interacting with you, you have an amazing ability to build on that relationship to offer a broader set of products.

An Internet business is not like a bank branch where you can train employees on only a small number of products. The virtual nature of the Internet enables whatever shopping your customers want to do. You'll see more companies like Amazon, that are strong in one online area and then expand their product offerings. The warning to every business is that even if no one in your industry jumps in early, big online companies, trying to cover every commercial area, will move into yours.

Learn about the Internet today. Find some of your customers who are already adopting the Web lifestyle. Use this group to develop models for how you might do business overall. Within a decade most of your other customers will have made the shift, and you'll be prepared.

The middleman must add value

Here at the start of the twenty-first century, a basic new rule of business is that the Internet changes everything. Internet technologies are altering the way every company, even a small one, deals with its employees, partners, and suppliers.

Not every company needs to use the Internet to interact with its customers right now, but soon a company website where customers can do business with the firm will be as essential as the telephone and a mailing address have been. Already the great majority of Fortune 500 companies have websites. The Internet is reducing costs and changing the relationships of companies with their customers. The Internet produces more competition among sellers and helps sellers to find possible customers.

In pre-Internet days, the only way customers could get goods from most manufacturers was through layers of middlemen.

Today customers can do business directly with manufacturers eager to offer Internet service. Today any manufacturer can provide the Internet version of a factory store.

Before the Internet, gathering all the information for financial services, travel options, and other products required lots of time. Huge numbers of service companies made their money by collecting and organizing that kind of information for customers. Today, despite search tools that aren't perfect, customers can go to the Internet to find much more of the information they need. And any company can provide valuable information cheaply on the Internet, without branch offices.

In 1995, in *The Road Ahead*, I described how the Internet is helping to create Adam Smith's ideal market, in which buyers and sellers can easily find one another without taking much time or spending much money. The first problem in most markets is finding someone to do business with. The second problem is understanding the nature and quality of the goods and services that are being offered. The Internet makes it easy for a buyer to get background information about a product and to compare prices easily. Buyers can also tell sellers more about what they require, and sellers will be able to target their goods at the people who are most interested in them and sell related products.

The Internet is a great tool for helping customers to find the best deal they can. It is quite easy for buyers to jump from one website to another to find the best prices on some goods. At least two different services provide price comparisons for customers shopping for goods such as books and CDs. Some travel sites feature automated bargain finders that can find low air fares. At least one company, priceline.com, reverses the buyer–seller relationship by having buyers bid the price they're willing to pay for a car or a plane ticket and offering that price to various sellers. It is unclear yet how broadly this approach will be used, but it is possible only through the Internet.

Over time, software will automate price comparisons even more, until they become effortlessly electronic. At least one online store already checks other major sites for the prices of commonly purchased items and automatically reduces its prices to make sure that they're always slightly lower. Without stores to pay for, the seller may still make a profit. Customers will be able to join together electronically to get lower prices in ways that have not been easy before. There will even be cases in which software representing the seller negotiates with software representing hundreds or thousands of customers.

For the majority of products which are available through many stores, customers will benefit most. For unique products and services, sellers will find more possible customers and may charge higher prices. The more customers adopt the Web lifestyle, the closer the economy will move toward Adam Smith's perfect market in all areas of commerce.

Customers can now deal directly with manufacturers and service providers, so there is little value added in simply transferring goods or information. Various people have predicted "the death of the middleman." Certainly the value of some kinds of middleman is quickly falling to zero. Travel agents who simply book air fares will disappear. This kind of high-volume, low-value dealing is perfect for a self-service Internet travel site. In the future travel agents will need to do more than book tickets; they will need to create a total travel adventure. A travel agent who provides highly personalized tours of Italy or the California wine country will still be in great demand.

If you're a middleman, the Internet's promise of cheaper prices and faster service can end your role of assisting the contact between the producer and the customer. If this is happening to you, one option is to use the Internet to get back into the action. That's what Egghead, a major chain of software stores, did after struggling for several years. Egghead closed all of its physical stores in 1998 and began selling just on the Internet. Egghead now offers a number of new online programs that take advantage of the Internet, such as electronic sales for about fifty different categories of hardware and software, and for used computers. It's not yet clear whether Egghead will succeed and meet the test described in this chapter, which is that the middleman must add value, but the company certainly understands the principle.

Every store needs to take the Internet into account. The success of the Amazon.com bookstore, which exists only on the Internet, caused Barnes & Noble to combine its successful physical bookstores with a strong online presence, and to start working with Bertelsmann, a leading international media company.

For service industries, the Internet requires you to be either a high-volume, low-cost provider, or a provider of highly personalized services. For the high-volume, low-cost model, you use Internet technology to create a self-service approach. You make a lot of information available to customers and you drive a lot of traffic through your Internet site by offering the best price. Because only a few companies in any market will be the high-volume players, most companies will have to find ways to use the Internet not just to reduce costs, but also to deliver new services.

E * Trade Securities started low-cost finance services on the Internet in 1992. By 1998 at least seventy companies bought and sold shares for their customers online, and the number was going up. Finance firms that still offer a service face-to-face or over the phone have a problem: most of the data about shares that these companies provide for their customers is available free on the Internet. But if the companies that do not offer an Internet service become electronic traders (e-traders), what can they do that is different to what customers are already offered?

Merrill Lynch, the market-leading finance company, asked itself exactly that question when it looked at the way it did business in 1997. Customers have invested with Merrill Lynch for more than a century. The company has managed their shares by getting large amounts of financial data, analyzing it, and making long-term financial plans. By 1997 customers had more than one trillion dollars invested with Merrill Lynch. But the growth of low-cost trading and then Internet-based trading between 1992 and 1997 showed managers that the company would have to change. As Howard Sorgen of Merrill Lynch said, "Our customers were changing. The way people got information and made decisions was changing. We would have been foolish to think we didn't have to change, too."

Merrill Lynch's main assets are its financial consultants, the people who advise clients about their investments. But in 1997 they were spending a lot of their time finding data and not enough time advising clients about their investments. The information systems at that time were expensive and hard to use. All the different categories of data—share prices, product information, the customer database, pricing—were on different systems, and all of them were incompatible and difficult to use. The new information system was built round the financial consultants. It helped them get data and develop the best financial plan for the client as quickly as possible. To save money and development time the company also wanted to use existing products when possible.

Merrill Lynch managers asked their board for a billion dollars to invest in new technology. The board agreed that the best way to compete was to give the company's knowledge workers—the financial consultants—the best knowledge tools. So the managers got permission for what became a five year, $825 million project. This was completed on time in October 1998 for close to the $825 million estimate. Of that cost, about $250 million went on software development. Much of the remaining expense—a system for getting share prices and market news, for example—

would have been required whatever software Merrill Lynch used. The actual difference in cost was about $250 million over four years. For slightly more than $60 million a year, approximately $3,500 per financial consultant, Merrill Lynch improved the information system for the 14,700 financial consultants in its 700 US offices and for another 2,000 consultants internationally.

Chief Technical Officer Howard Sorgen showed me the Merrill Lynch solution. All systems are now fully compatible. All financial information, from any source, is organized into " pages " and then " books." The financial consultant can look anywhere in these books—at share prices on NASDAQ, New York, and Tokyo, for example. The financial consultant can see immediately if all the client's shares are doing well or badly and why. Before, this took a lot of time as shares in each company were looked at individually. Now, the financial consultant can even see immediately what would happen if one lot of shares was bought and another sold. Soon clients will be able to see these calculations on their own PC screens. Also, the system behaves like a well-trained assistant to the financial controller. If the controller's client has shares in a company, the system will put background data about the company on the screen without being asked, whenever the controller asks for the share price.

Since the changes in the system at Merrill Lynch, financial consultants have more time to build stronger relationships with clients. Merrill Lynch then decided that giving more information to clients would make the relationship with them stronger, not weaker.

Merrill Lynch Online is a version of the Merrill Lynch system for customers. It gives the customer some background data on which decisions are based, and it also has basic information about the client's account with Merrill Lynch. The company hoped to get 200,000 customers in the first year, an average of about 550 people a day. Instead, 700 to 800 people a day went online with the system. One surprise was the age of the customers who took the system first. Merrill Lynch thought that the younger customers who had grown up with the Internet would try the system first, but the older, wealthier clients were the first customers.

After the first success, Merrill Lynch added more to the online service. Today, customers can e-mail their financial consultants, look at the latest share prices, and buy and sell shares. Merrill Lynch now see the Internet as an opportunity, not a threat. It gives the client information, but financial information is not financial knowledge. That is still provided by the financial consultants, who now have more time to concentrate on it. And they provide it to well-informed clients, who ask better questions than badly-informed clients. The aim now is to have the client and the financial consultant looking at the same data on screen at the same time. Then, as Merrill Lynch people like to say, " the real magic starts."

Touch your customers

As electronic commerce grows, not only middlemen will find creative ways to use the Internet to strengthen their relationships with customers. The businesses that treat e-commerce as more than a way to easy money will do the best. Sales are the final goal, of course, but the sale itself is only one part of the online customer experience. Some companies will use the Internet to interact with their customers in ways that haven't been possible before. They will make the sale part of a series of customer services for which the Internet has unique strengths.

It's important that customers come away from electronic interactions pleased enough to tell their friends. This is the most powerful means by which any product or company builds a reputation, and the Internet is a medium made for easy communication. If a customer doesn't like a product or the way a trader has treated him, he's likely to e-mail all of his friends. An Internet car site called Autoweb.com asks customers about dealer service by e-mail, and removes dealers from its lists if they fail to improve their service as a result of complaints.

Today, the main competition for online stores is physical stores. Physical stores have much higher sales volumes than online stores. Online sales in 1998 were only 0.5 percent of the total sales in the world's seven largest economies. But that percentage will grow enormously in the next decade. As e-commerce takes off, the main competition for Internet sites will no longer be physical stores but other online stores.

Rapidly growing categories for online commerce include finance and insurance, travel, and computer sales. Companies such as Cisco Systems, Dell Computer, and Microsoft are now doing billions of dollars each in business over the Internet every year. Chrysler expects its 1.5 percent online sales volume to jump to 25 percent in four years. Even the most cautious estimates project an annual growth rate of about 45 percent for online sales. The highest estimates were for more than $1.6 trillion in business by the year 2000. I think this is too low.

Dell was one of the first big companies to move into e-commerce. The company supplies computers worldwide, selling more than $18 billion worth of products. It began selling its products online in mid-1996. Its online business quickly rose from $1 million a week to $1 million a day. Soon it jumped to $3 million a day and then $5 million. It is still rising. Computer buyers clearly like and find it easy to buy their computers on the Web. At the time of writing, Dell has more than 1.5 million visits a week to its website, and 11 percent of its business is online. Dell hoped that this would grow to 50 percent, maybe as early as 2000.

Michael Dell, who started the company, believes in direct selling and computer-aided commerce. But he knows that the

Internet has to be a basic part of the overall business strategy. Dell's entire business is based on online commerce and support. Dell's first site provided product information, let customers buy online, and asked for customer ideas. Dell learned a lot from the suggestions that came in, mainly online. Over time Dell has made hundreds of changes to its website. Customers can do more and more online. They can now see online the progress of the product they have ordered.

"The Internet doesn't replace people. It makes them more efficient," says Michael Dell. "We had to build an Internet system that was so convenient, customers got more value for their time than they did on the phone."

Having more information online for customers didn't reduce the value of Dell's sales team. Like Merrill Lynch, Dell found out that an educated customer is a better customer. Dell's sales team became more like consultants to the customer. And they have more time for consulting because buying and selling online is so much quicker.

One of Dell's unique approaches to customer support was to create more than 5,000 individually designed pages for its big customers. About 65 percent of Dell's online business is from individuals and small businesses, and the Premier pages are one way that Dell is growing its corporate business. They make large purchases online easier and quicker.

Only Information Technology (IT) can balance the need to keep enough stock to supply customers quickly with the cost of keeping too much stock. Perfect information about what the customer needs is the answer to the need for zero stock waiting for an order.

◆

Marriott International, the world's largest hotel company, earns more than $10 billion from its 1,500 hotels around the world under ten different brands. The hotels have had an online booking system since 1996, and although Marriott says the system was simple and just an experiment, it did $1 million in business by the end of the year.

Marriott saw that the Internet could do even more, and in early 1997 they created a special Internet team. From the start, the technology team worked closely with the business team. Studies showed that one of the subjects people wanted information about most was travel. "The Internet is all about service," says Marriott's Mike Pusateri, "providing service to customers in a way that is faster, friendlier, and more personal than they or the company has ever experienced before. And service is Marriott's business."

Marriott was one of the first companies to build an interactive home page on its website. You can search online for a Marriott hotel by asking for hotels in a certain city, for hotels with certain facilities, and for hotels that have certain features in their rooms. Linked pages show attractions close to the hotel, for example a golf course. Or, if you want to go to a Chinese restaurant, the system will list the six nearest. When you have chosen your hotel, you can find out about prices and book a room. There are also links to other sites that book rooms, like TravelWeb.com and Microsoft Expedia.com. Marriott's site has links to 1,000 other webpages.

Because each visitor searches for exactly what he or she wants on the Marriott website, each visitor has a different experience. The website is visited by 15,000 people a day, which brought in more than $2 million a month in money from Internet sources in 1997. It's hard for Marriott to know what percentage of this return would have come in anyway, by traditional methods, but it is clear that the Internet is attracting wealthier customers who prefer its more expensive hotels. On average, an online customer spends more with Marriott than the average customer.

Marriott has found, as others have found, that the more interactive a site is, the more business activity it gets from its visitors. For example, instead of floor plans future customers see virtual pictures of the hotel. Soon customers will be able to enter the place they want to stay and the names of other Marriott hotels they have stayed in. The site will then give them the nearest Marriott hotel that is like the hotel they enjoyed before.

Marriott does not cut out middlemen, it makes them part of its customer service. The company provides special places on its website for travel agents and meeting planners. Thousands of meeting planners view the Marriott site because they don't have to visit the hotel before they make a decision on where to have their meeting.

Adopt the Web lifestyle

If you asked your friends why they use the phone to communicate with their friends, or why they turn to the television for entertainment or breaking news, they'd look at you in a strange way. If you asked your friends whether they'd adopted " the electricity lifestyle," they'd think you were crazy.

People in developed countries don't think much about their electrical products; we just use them. But people who are now in their fifties can remember when just a few families had TVs. Our grandparents can remember when much of rural America was without electricity. It's taken more than a hundred years for the electricity lifestyle to revolutionize civilization.

When streets and houses were first wired, the only use for electricity was for lighting. Electricity's capacity to change everyone's lifestyle was hidden. Electric light was cleaner, safer, brighter, and more convenient than natural gas, oil, or candles. When the infrastructure was in place, though, new products were

36

created that took advantage of electricity. Electric refrigerators, record players, and air conditioners applied the new technology to existing needs. The most revolutionary uses of electricity were the phone, the radio, and the TV. These new machines changed our economies and our lifestyles. People hadn't dreamed of these products before the infrastructure was available.

Because the Internet is a communications infrastructure that depends on electricity, you could say that its popular acceptance is an extension of the electricity lifestyle. But the Internet is enabling a new way of life that I call "the Web lifestyle." The Web lifestyle, like the electricity lifestyle, will be characterized by new things happening quickly. The infrastructure for high-speed communications is producing new software and hardware that will change people's lives.

Intelligent machines such as the PC are becoming more powerful and less expensive. Since they are programmable, they can be used for many different tasks. Within a decade most Americans and many other people around the world will be living the Web lifestyle. It will be natural for these people to turn to the Web to get news, to learn, to be entertained, and to communicate. It will be just as normal as picking up the phone to talk to somebody or to order something. The Web will be used to pay your bills, manage your finances, communicate with your doctor, and do any business. Just as naturally, you'll carry one or more small machines using a radio connection to stay constantly in touch and do electronic business wherever you are.

For a lot of people the Web lifestyle is very close today. By 1998 more than sixty million Americans were using the Web regularly, up from twenty-two million the year before. By 1998 the average user went on the Web eight to nine separate times a month, spending a total of about three and a half hours a month online. It's exciting to see that people living the Web lifestyle are using the Internet to learn and buy in new ways. When the

Sojourner landed on Mars in the summer of 1997, NASA's*
website had forty-seven million hits in four days from people
seeking more detail than they could get from the traditional news
media.

Businesses are providing a wide variety of information and
services, like real-time stock quotes, sports scores, and city guides.
You can buy almost anything on the Web, from paintings to old
toys. The Web is an ideal vehicle for helping to build a
community, too. There are sites for tracking missing children, for
helping people adopt pets, and for every pastime that you can
imagine. Sites that involve citizens are getting excellent traffic
flow.

A cultural change as significant as a move to the Web lifestyle
will depend on the age of users to some degree. The kids
growing up with the new technology will show us the full
possibilities. Personal computer use, high-speed networks, and
online communication are widespread. Universities are getting
rid of paper forms and registering students for classes over the
Web. Students can look at their grades and even send in work
over the Web. Teachers hold online discussion groups. Students
e-mail friends and family as naturally as they call them on the
phone.

The adoption of technology for the Web lifestyle is happening
faster than the adoption of electricity, cars, TV, and radio. Many
people who use PCs at the office install them at home for work,
and then use them for much more. A lot of people over fifty-five
years old, who wouldn't usually add new technology to their
lifestyle, want to use the Internet as a way to stay in touch with
their friends and families. Revolutionary new uses of the Internet
that none of us can accurately predict today will change the

*NASA: the North American Space Agency runs the US space program.

world as completely in the twenty-first century as the unexpected uses of electricity did in the twentieth—and faster.

As people move rapidly online, one of the most basic changes will be the degree to which customers will manage their finances online. In 1998 only about one million of the fifteen billion total bills in the United States were paid electronically. Little online customer service was available. In fact, though customers can pay some bills online, in almost every case they still receive them on paper. When customers are able to pay online, the US Commerce Department estimates, processing costs will drop more than $20 billion annually. Today you have to calculate on paper what bills you want to pay and how much you want to pay on each. In the future, software will enable you to calculate online the effect of various payments on your bank balance. You'll make your payment exactly when it's due. And bill payment software will communicate with financial management software.

By late 1998 about half of all American homes had PCs, and about half of those PCs were connected to the Web. The percentages are lower in most other countries. Reducing the cost of high-speed communications so people can remain constantly connected, and making the software easier to use, are essential to making the Web lifestyle common. I believe that by the year 2001 more than 60 percent of US homes will have PCs and that 85 percent of those homes will be online. For other countries to reach these levels of use they will have to invest heavily in communications infrastructure.

People don't realize how much the hardware and software will improve. Take just one example: screen technology. I do my electronic mail on a fifty-centimeter flat screen. It's not available at a reasonable price yet, but in two or three years it will be. In five years a hundred-centimeter flat screen will be affordable. Screen quality will have a big effect on how much people will read on the screen instead of on paper.

The cost of a personal computer is also coming down. Historically, the PC industry has concentrated on creating a more powerful PC at a particular price. Now advances are reducing prices as well. Capable PCs cost much less than $1,000 today, and lower prices are expanding the market. Looking at a ten-year time frame, you're going to have PCs that cost the same as a typical TV. In fact, the difference between a TV and a PC will be small because even the boxes that connect TVs to the cable system will have a processor more powerful than the one we have today in the most expensive PC.

Smaller personal companions will become common. These will include the small PCs on the market today, and new PCs that are the size of a wallet, which will enable electronic operations. The phone, radio, and TV will pick up new capabilities as they go digital. Some machines will be carried with you. Some will be in different rooms in your house. Others will become standard in vehicles.

Any of them will enable you to use e-mail and voice mail, get information from stock reports or other news, and find out the latest weather and news of your flight. These machines will connect through wires or through technologies that don't use wires, such as radio. Though the machines will operate independently, they will exchange data among themselves automatically.

These machines will become part of ordinary life. When you leave the office for the day, your personal digital companion will download your e-mail, which might include a grocery list from your husband or wife. At the store, you can download a new recipe, and all of the items for the meal will be added to your list. Your digital companion is smart enough to speak to all the machines that need to know your home or work schedule, but only tells the kitchen machines about the recipe. From a computer in the kitchen, you check the house. A video of the front door area shows who called when no one was home.

Digital security cameras connected to a network are becoming cheaper and will be common to reduce theft. Some schools are providing cameras to enable parents to check on their kids while they're at school.

While dinner is cooking, you go to a private website for your extended family, and find out that everyone has been in the chat room discussing what to do when the family meets. They used electronic voting to choose half a dozen possible events, and they've asked you to book as many of them as you can. A software agent, which knows you have already booked travel for the trip, suggests several things to do locally, including sailing, which was on your family's list. The agent also tells you about a new, lower air fare to your destination. You digitally book the sailing and the lower fares.

When you're ready to watch TV, you might look at the electronic programming guide on screen or use another software agent to see what's on. You've told the agent your viewing tastes and it's tracked your actual viewing patterns, so it recommends several shows among the hundreds available on digital TV. You choose to see a football game. While watching, you use the interactive menu to enter a contest and to vote for the most valuable player. Viewer scores will count for half the final result. You watch a commercial advertising a car. Most viewers see a commercial for a truck, but data that you have volunteered through your TV indicates that you're a better candidate for a family vehicle.

Development of intelligent, interactive TV will come as television moves to digital technology. Digital broadcasts are easy to correct for errors, and allow high-quality video and sound. Digital TV can do a lot more than improve broadcast quality, though. Satellite and cable companies are already using digital TV to deliver more channels. Over time, the biggest effect of digital TV will come from the ability to include other digital data, providing interactivity, intelligent software, targeted advertising and sales offers, and the Web.

Broadcasters will provide greater content such as links to relevant websites or entirely new Web content that adds to the broadcast, or music, or software that can be downloaded for a fee. Many of the new features require a two-way link, which is easy for the new cable TV systems. New technology will make the TV interface easier. Trying to record one or more programs at certain times and days remains annoyingly complex. In the future, taping a show will be as simple as telling the TV exactly what you want to tape. Using speech to interact with the TV, PC, or other personal companions will be common within ten years.

Bandwidth, the information-carrying capacity of a digital communications system, remains the biggest barrier to the widespread adoption of the Web lifestyle in all countries. Bandwidth is also the biggest cost. In developed nations businesses can generally afford the bandwidth they need to work digitally because lots of communications companies are wiring business districts. But it will take much longer to get affordable wiring into homes, schools, and libraries, which is critical to achieving a fully connected society. We will only see the benefits of a Web lifestyle when high-bandwidth systems are in place. The most important step for a country to achieve a high-bandwidth infrastructure is to encourage competition in the communications industry.

Scientists all over the world are exploring new communications technologies—and old ones. Recently a British engineer developed a way to send high-speed voice and data signals on ordinary electrical current, raising the possibility that Internet service could one day ride into your home over our existing infrastructure of electrical wires. This and other technologies such as satellite broadcasting are exciting because they don't require us to replace the existing wiring that already connects most homes in the developed world. It's a huge task to get the Web infrastructure in place all over the world, but the advances in many areas make it likely that the speed of improvement will surprise everyone in the next decade.

The social effects of the Web lifestyle will be enormous. A lot of people fear that computers and the Internet will make life less personal, creating a world that's less warm and friendly. Some people were afraid, at first, that the telephone would reduce face-to-face contact, too. Two people might call each other when they would have talked face-to-face without the phone, and two people might e-mail each other when they would have met face-to-face without e-mail.

Any medium can be misused. The development of personal and professional manners for the Web will continue. It's easy enough to say that the Web lifestyle, with everyone in his or her little world, will cause society to fly apart. I believe the opposite is actually true. Just as the phone and e-mail have increased contact between people living in different communities, the PC and the Internet give us another way to communicate. They don't take any away.

In reality, the ability to use the Internet to move or change the boundaries of our communities is strengthening personal and cultural connections. The city of Amsterdam, in the Netherlands, has Internet discussions about issues like city planning, safety, and drugs. Citizens can connect to the police by e-mail. An Egyptian site for children called the Little Horus website contains more than 300 pages of information and pictures covering Egypt's 7,000 years of civilization. It also has information about Egypt today, including its economic, cultural, and social life. The " Tour " section includes tips on popular destinations for children.

The Web lifestyle is about broadening horizons, not narrowing them. Building communities is going to be one of the biggest growth areas in the next few years on the Web. The Web dramatically increases the number of communities you can join.

In the past you might have had time to be a part of your neighborhood community and one or two social organizations. In the Web lifestyle you are limited only by your interests.

One of the most powerful effects of the Web is the way it can connect groups of people independent of geography or time zones. If you want to get together a group of enthusiastic card players or talk about issues with people who share your political views, the Web makes it easy to do. If you want to follow what's happening in your hometown, the Web can help.

How are we going to find the time to live a Web lifestyle and join more communities? The Web will make things more efficient than they used to be. You can quickly find out how much your used car is worth, plan a trip, or find out anything you need to know when you want to make a major purchase. These things are easy on the Web today. And people will probably trade some of the time they now spend reading the paper or watching TV for the information or entertainment they'll find on the Web. A British study in 1998 showed that about 25 percent of the British adults who used the Internet watched less television than they did before.

◆

Much of this book is about having all the information we want at the tips of our fingers. Most people want to find the best price for a product or to be up-to-date on the important issues affecting their local or national communities. We have managed without this information because obtaining it has simply been too difficult. The Web lifestyle isn't about changing human nature or the basics of how people live. Instead the Web lifestyle gives more people a chance to pursue their interests in a better way.

The Web lifestyle will change the way people shop. With the Web as the world's biggest collection of shopping malls, customers will have choices they didn't have before. They'll be able to find all the choices for goods they want and, in many cases, have them specially made. They can have the final product delivered directly to their doors. Because customers are demanding faster and more personal service, and stronger relationships, the Web lifestyle will drive companies to develop a digital nervous system in order to stay with their competitors.

The Web connects workers, friends, and families in new ways. Communities based on shared interests are forming with members from all over the world. Governments have the chance to involve citizens more than ever before. By enabling people to shop, get news, meet one another, be entertained, and gossip in ways we're only now beginning to understand, the Internet is becoming the town square for the village that the world will be tomorrow.

With a Web lifestyle, people can overcome many of the barriers that have existed for so long that we almost take them for granted. The Web lifestyle is not about adding complexity to already busy lives. As people become accustomed to the Web lifestyle, they'll eventually accept it unthinkingly, just as they do the electricity lifestyle they live today.

Change the boundaries of business

A flow of digital information changes the way people, organizations, and businesses work. Internet technologies will also change the boundaries of organizations of all sizes. In changing the boundaries, the "Web workstyle" of using digital tools and processes enables both organizations and individuals to change their roles. A corporation can use the Internet to work smoothly with professionals such as lawyers and accountants who remain "outside" the company walls. An important reengineering principle is that companies should concentrate on their basic skills and outsource everything else. The Internet allows a company to do this to a greater extent than ever before by changing which employees work within the walls and which work outside in a different role.

Our basic skills at Microsoft are creating high-volume software products, working with other software companies, and providing customer service and support. We outsource a number of functions that don't fall into those categories, from help-desk technical support for our employees to the physical production of our software packages. The Web workstyle makes it possible to deal better with unpredictable demand. Because you have a great need for a skill, and then you don't, for some areas you want to be able to hire staff for a short time to deal with peaks and valleys. The Internet means that more companies can take a "studio" approach to running major parts of their businesses. Big Hollywood studios have full-time employees to handle finance, marketing, and other continuous projects, but the creative side of the business, the full-time movie-making staff, isn't very big at all. When a movie concept is agreed upon, a director brings together a large group of people to create the film. When they're finished, they move on to other projects.

Web technology makes it possible for many different kinds of projects to be structured as studio-type work. A project owner who wants to hire a team can go online, describe the project, and find out who's available. People and organizations with the right skills can declare their interest, and the project owner can build a team quickly. People looking for work will find more opportunities for employment that meets their particular interests and needs—if they have highly specialized skills, for example, or if they want to work only certain hours.

Despite these changes, big firms won't break themselves down into project-by-project production companies. Big companies will continue to balance the load of their work as they always have—they'll just use technology to do it more efficiently. Every company will experiment to find its most efficient size and organizational structure, though the trend will be toward smaller companies. Medium-size and small companies can take advantage of the boundary-changing possibilities of the Web to act much bigger than they are, without adding employees or offices. A small company with the right skills can bid on and lead a movie production, a construction job, or an advertising project. By joining with other companies and professionals quickly, it can act as a virtual large company to work on the project until its profitable end. Because the team can be broken up at the end of the project, the company can manage labor resources without the administrative burden of a large full-time staff.

Some employees in companies of any size are naturally nervous about the effects of the Web workstyle. They assume that if their company chooses to build itself around Web technologies, their jobs may disappear. They won't—unless "restructuring" is just a fancy term to hide sackings. When a company downsizes, jobs are lost. When a company outsources, jobs move. The goal is not to get rid of work, but to move the responsibility to specialists outside. It's much more efficient for many companies, including Microsoft, to have an outside company handle installation and support for small computers, for example, because companies that specialize in such work can develop world-best skills and because we can ask for competitive bids for the job.

Employees who react to the possibility of outsourcing with fear are assuming that work belongs "in" the company and not "out." As companies change, some people will have difficulties. Despite the understandable anxiety, employees should also look at the changes as opportunities to define their jobs the way they want them, and to work for an organization of the size and personality they prefer. They can even use this revolution as a chance to start their own business. Not long ago, one person who had been a writer watched Microsoft outsource writing work and recognized an opportunity. Today this person has a fine business managing a dozen or more writers, and Microsoft staff spend their time defining the work to be done instead of trying to manage the writing process for a bunch of different people. Overall the changes in organizational structure will be good for good employees.

The Web workstyle is particularly well-suited to lawyers, doctors, accountants, and engineers, who usually work independently or in small teams. One of the reasons professionals have traditionally organized themselves into firms is to deal with the rises and falls of customer demand. Now, instead of joining together to make sure the workload is shared, they'll also have the choice of working on their own and using the Internet to find customers.

Not everyone will choose this approach. A lot of people want to work for bigger firms. They like the idea of belonging to one company, working on long-term projects, and being part of the community and culture of a particular workplace. They invest in their career, and the company invests in them. A lot of the most interesting jobs, such as software design at my company, are central areas that won't be outsourced. Most companies, including Microsoft, work hard to make it attractive for good employees to stay long-term. Developers join Microsoft because they see the chance to design software or develop technologies that will be used by millions of people. Like many artists, they want their work to reach the largest possible audience.

People who want to work for a big company will work for one, and people who don't want to will have interesting alternatives. A Web workstyle also makes it easier for people who have good skills but who can't, or choose not to, work full time. Because they can find more work over the Internet, and do more work from home, those people will have new opportunities. Society will benefit by making better use of this huge pool of talent.

As a business manager, you need to take a hard look at your basic skills. Look again at the areas of your company that aren't directly involved in that work, and consider whether Web technologies can enable you to outsource those tasks. Let another company take over the management responsibilities for that work and use modern communications technology to work closely with the people—now partners instead of employees—doing the work. Also, consider the employees who have good skills and experience, but decide they don't want to work full time. Better communication tools may allow you to continue using these people. The competition to hire the best people will increase in the years ahead. Companies that give extra freedom to their employees will have the advantage in this key area.

Get to market first

Customers want high-quality products at low prices, and they want them now. Every business, whether it's a producer of products and services or a supplier to that producer, has to react quickly while keeping quality high and price low. Information technology has become a major contributor to the faster responses, the higher quality, and the lower price rises that have defined business in the last decade.

Few industries illustrate the two main pressures of shrinking time and improving quality better than the car industry. Japanese car designs in the 1980s appeared fresher and their quality improvements more frequent than in American cars because Japanese car makers could take a car from concept to mass production in three years. American car makers typically took four to six years, and their costs were higher.

American companies responded by breaking down the organizational barriers that had divided design, manufacturing, and sales divisions from one another. They also improved communications with their external partners. Designers, engineers, suppliers, and manufacturing personnel began to work in tight teams that communicated electronically, cutting the time from product design to salesroom floor by half.

Other process improvements in the car industry have been significantly helped by technology, including the computer-aided design (CAD) of cars. The 3-D modeling capacities of CAD programs enable engineers to design a vehicle without having to build a model by hand first. The designers can see whether parts will fit together and can change part designs without building special tools. Electronic links between car manufacturers and suppliers have already reduced the error rate in parts delivered by 72 percent, and saved up to eight hours per week per car in labor costs.

Customers have benefited from better cars, produced more quickly. Ford's achievements in production are representative of the entire car industry. In 1990 the company took five or more years to take a car from concept to customer, and it experienced 150 faults for every 100 cars, or 1.5 faults per car. By 1998 Ford had cut its cycle time by more than half, to less than twenty-four months. Its fault rate had gone down from 150 to 81 faults per 100 cars.

In some industries the issue is getting to market fast when change is more and more complex. Intel, for example, has always had a ninety-day production cycle for its chips, which power most PCs. Intel expects to maintain this ninety-day production rate, although the processor is getting more and more complex. The number of transistors in the chip increased from 29,000 in the 8086 chip to 7.5 million in the Pentium in 1998, and what the processor is capable of grew by 10,000 in the same twenty years. By 2011 Intel expects to deliver chips that have one billion transistors. Moore's law says that the power of the chips doubles every eighteen to twenty-four months. If cars and cereal went the same way, then by Moore's law a car would cost twenty-seven dollars and a box of cereal would cost a penny.

Intel uses a variety of management, production, and digital methods to maintain efficiency while putting more and more transistors onto a chip the size of a thumbnail. Each time the production process changes, new factories are built that cost more than a billion dollars each.

In 1998 Intel introduced a "copy exactly" strategy to maintain the same level of efficiency and quality across all its chip factories. A program called D2000 made sure that every design engineer got the benefit of best practice across the organization. Intel discovered that more than 60 percent of the problems the designers faced had already been solved by another design team. It's very likely that any large company using manual processes would find a similar amount of repeated work. D2000 has helped Intel to almost double the speed of new product production since 1994, and it has helped Intel toward its goal of volume production from the first design of a chip, without having to go through several versions of a design to get it right.

Although banks have always been big users of information technology, they have not had a reputation for fast time to market with new products or services, except for Banco Bradesco, the largest bank in Brazil. With nearly 2,200 branches and twenty million customers, Banco Bradesco has $68.7 billion in assets and serves three million people a day. It was the first Brazilian bank to use computers in 1962, and it was the first bank to offer automated cash machines, in 1982. Banco Bradesco uses technology to stay ahead of the competition. Even six months is too long to bring an idea to the market; the usual development cycle is weeks or, at most, a few months. The bank also aims to bring a new product or service to its entire customer base at the same time.

For one small-business customer, Bradesco developed software to assist with money going into and out of the business. Now about 4,100 businesses are using this program. For another customer, Bradesco developed a salary card that employees could use in a Bradesco cash machine, even if they did not have an account with the bank. The card is now in use at about 1,300 companies and will soon be in use at 2,000 companies with one million employees. In each case, Bradesco was the first bank to offer the service.

In 1996, Banco Bradesco became the first bank in Brazil, and only the fifth in the world, to use the Internet to offer banking services. By 1998 the number of online customers was growing at 12 percent per month. Online banking is more popular in Brazil than in any other country. The bank's website, BradescoNet, offers a full range of financial services. By being the first important commercial Internet site in Brazil, the bank has the opportunity to become the site that Brazilians go through to get to other sites. What better way to keep customers loyal to your company?

But the bank recognizes that it needs to use its digital nervous system even better in the future. The bank wants to collect more information about each customer so that it can sell new financial products targeted at the right people. For example, if a program finds a customer paying car insurance, the bank could offer a loan to buy a new car, even if the customer financed his present car at another bank. Customer data is one of the bank's best assets. It will take Bradesco several years to put together all the information they have, but when they do they can offer many more financial services targeted at the right people.

Time to market has got faster in the PC industry than anywhere else. In this situation a better flow of digital information does not just improve the company, it is essential for the company's success.

In just a few years the product cycle for Compaq computers dropped from eighteen months to twelve months. By late 1998 it dropped to six to nine months for business products and to four months for consumer products. But with its older information systems, Compaq needed forty-five days to collect its worldwide sales information and reduce it to the single set of numbers needed for product planning. By the time it could communicate its manufacturing needs to its suppliers, the company would be halfway through the four-month product lifecycle for important products.

Compaq started an Enterprise Resource Planning (ERP)* system. All its factories now use the same software, so all the data that goes into ERP is compatible. The forty-five day planning cycle has now come down to a week. Although a week's sales are necessary to see long-term sales trends, in the future it will have data on sales per day.

Compaq is also using real-time systems which help it to react to unplanned changes in demand. Using the same data that goes into ERP, Compaq wants to look at its supply and order position three times a night, eight hours apart in the United States, Europe, and Asia. With real-time data instead of data that is a week or even a day old, Compaq wants to be able to see and react to, for example, an unplanned order for 7,000 PCs, and work with suppliers to see immediately if the company can deliver the order in time.

To be able to move as quickly as possible as a company, Compaq has moved all its data systems onto the Internet. An e-commerce system means that when an order comes in, the supplier sees this at the same time as the Compaq planner. But all this has to be done while production is still going on. John White, Chief Information Officer of Compaq in 1998, said it was like changing the wings and engine of a jet while it was still flying.

*ERP: a program that tracks every stage of the manufacture of a product.

Another software decision is: do you get all the ERP software from one company or do you get the best from a lot of different companies? Because compatibility is so important, most companies are going to a single company for all their ERP needs. But Microsoft is interested in making ERP work either across versions or with one set of software. Compaq's solutions are a good example of how technology and business depend on each other, and help each other.

Digital processes make it possible for every company to dramatically shorten its time to market, although some amount of time and energy will always be required to deliver physical goods. MIT's Nicholas Negroponte describes the difference between physical products and information products in the digital age as the difference between moving atoms around (physical products such as cars and computers) and moving bits[*] around (electronic products such as financial analyses and news broadcasts). Producers of bits can use the Internet to reduce their delivery times to almost zero. Producers of atoms still can't do this, but they can use bit-speed—digital organization of all kinds—to bring reaction time down dramatically. Almost all the time involved in producing an item is in the organization of the work, not in the actual production.

Good information systems can remove most of that waiting time. And makers of physical products will find that online service will become as much a part of their "product" and customer experience as the physical goods they deliver. The speed of delivery and the interaction with the customer made possible by the Internet effectively shifts products into services. Product companies today need to compare themselves not with the best of their competitors, but with the best of all service companies.

[*]bits: units of digital information.

In the end, the most important speed issue for companies is cultural. It's changing what everybody assumes about how rapidly they must move. Everybody must realize that if you don't satisfy customer demand quickly enough, without lowering quality, a competitor will. When people accept the need for action, digital technology enables a fast response.

Chapter 3   Manage Knowledge to Improve Strategic Thought

Bad news must travel fast

I have a natural ability to find bad news. If it's out there, I want to know about it. The people who work for me have realized this and keep me informed.

A lot goes wrong in any organization, even a good one. A product fails. You're surprised by a customer who suddenly switches to another company. A competitor brings out a product that appeals to a broad new market. Losing market share is the kind of bad news that every organization can understand. Other bad news may be about what's going on inside the company. Maybe a product is going to be late, or it's not going to do what you expected it to do, or you haven't been able to hire enough of the right kinds of people to carry out your plans. An essential quality of a good manager is the desire to seek bad news rather than deny it. An effective manager wants to hear about what's going wrong before he or she hears about what's going right. You can't react appropriately to disappointing news if it doesn't reach you soon enough.

You concentrate on bad news in order to get started on the solution quickly. As soon as you're aware of a problem, everybody in your organization must go into action. You can judge a company by how quickly it organizes all of its brain-power to deal with a serious problem. An important measure of a company's digital nervous system is how quickly people in the company find out about bad news and respond to it. Digital technology speeds business response time in any emergency.

In the old days, every company's response to bad news was slow. Business leaders often learned about problems only after they became serious, since the only quick way to pass information was to interrupt them with a phone call. Before handling a problem, people had to find information in paper files or go down the hall to find somebody who knew something about the situation. When people had some information, they spoke on the phone or sent papers to one another. Every step in the process took a lot of time. Today the dawn of the Information Age means we can send information fast, but even now most companies don't gather the key information about customer issues in one place. By contrast, a well-designed digital nervous system operates as an early-warning system.

◆

The Internet was not always Microsoft's top priority. Its arrival changed our business and became the biggest surprise we've ever had to respond to. In fact, in 1995 various experts said that the Internet would put Microsoft out of business. This was bad news on a huge scale. We used our digital nervous system to respond to that crisis.

On August 24, 1995, we introduced Windows 95, the most ambitious software product ever to reach the general customer. This was big news, and hundreds of stories appeared in the months before the release. *Windows* magazine said, "This year— for better or worse—Microsoft wins the war." A *Time* magazine story said that Microsoft was "the center of the computer universe." The introduction of Windows 95 itself was featured on major TV news broadcasts. Within a couple of months, though, the news stories were all taking the opposite view. The Internet had burst into the public's consciousness, and people believed that Microsoft hadn't been invited to the new party. Now stories in the press said we didn't understand the Internet. Smaller, quicker competitors would put Microsoft out of business.

On December 7, 1995, we held our first Internet Day, where for the first time we publicly displayed the range of technologies we were developing to build Internet support into our products. Within a year of this we had "Internet-enabled" our major products and delivered a number of new ones that concentrated on the Internet. Now we lead in several major Internet areas. No one company will dominate the Internet, but Microsoft has come back to play an important role.

How, our customers and the press often ask me, did we turn the ship around so fast? First, we were never so unaware of the Internet as we might have seemed to outside observers. It wasn't as if somebody said "Internet" and we didn't know how to spell it. We had several Internet technologies on our list of things to do. But let's also be clear. In 1993 we were not concentrating on the Internet. It was a fifth or sixth priority. At this time, we didn't have an overall Internet plan for the company. We didn't see that the Internet, a network for scientists and engineers, would grow into the worldwide commercial network it is today. The Internet had such a limited capacity to carry digital information then that we saw it as a minor stop along the way. The Internet's sudden growth in popularity changed all the rules. People knew the Internet had faults, but it made vast amounts of information available and enabled easy communication. In 1993 alone Internet use doubled to more than twenty-five million people.

The driving force behind Microsoft's response to the Internet didn't come from me or other senior executives. It came from a small number of enthusiastic employees who saw what was happening. Through our electronic systems they were able to get everybody to join them. Their story is an example of our practice, from day one, that smart people anywhere in the company should have the power to change things. It's an obvious way for Information Age companies to work: all knowledge workers should be part of creating the plan. But we couldn't make it work without the technology we use. For years everybody at Microsoft has had a PC with e-mail. It's a famous part of our company culture, and it's shaped the way we think and act.

We reached most of the important decisions during this crisis in face-to-face talk. But our decisions were all informed by exchanges taking place over e-mail. Working together electronically cannot replace face-to-face meetings. It's a way to make sure that more work gets done before meetings so that the meetings in person will be more useful. Meeting time is so valuable that you want to be sure you're dealing with facts and good ideas based on solid analysis. You want to be sure that meetings produce plans, that you don't just sit around talking philosophy. E-mail helps turn managers from middlemen into "doers." It encourages people to speak up. It encourages managers to listen. That's why, when customers ask what's the first thing they can do to get more value out of their information systems, I always answer, "e-mail."

How fast a company can respond in an emergency is a good measure of how well it responds to events. People in the organization will feel threatened by bad news, but that's OK if they feel it as a group. As a leader, I created a sense of crisis about the Internet in 1994 and 1995. Not to leave people unhappy or unable to work, but to excite them to action. The leader needs to create an environment in which people can analyze the situation and develop a good response.

I like good news as much as the next person, but it also makes me suspicious. I wonder what bad news I'm not hearing. When somebody sends me an e-mail about an account we've won, I always think, "There are a lot of accounts nobody has sent mail about. Does that mean we've lost all of those?"

This reaction may seem unnecessary, but I've found there's a psychological need in people to send good news when bad news is coming. It's as if they want to lessen the shock. A good e-mail system makes sure that bad news can travel fast, but your people have to be willing to send you the news. You must always be open to bad news, and then you have to act on it. Sometimes I think my most important job as a boss is to listen for bad news. If you don't act on it, your people will eventually stop bringing bad news to your attention. And that's the beginning of the end.

In three years every product my company makes will be out of date. The only question is whether we will replace them or someone else will. In the next ten years, if Microsoft remains a leader, we'll have to cope with at least three major crises. That's why we've always got to do better. I insist that we keep up with events, as well as pursue longer-term projects, and that we use "bad news" to drive us to put new features into our products. One day, somebody will catch us asleep. One day, a new firm will put Microsoft out of business. I just hope it's fifty years from now, not two or five.

Change bad news to good

If you treat unpleasant news not as a negative, but as evidence of a need for change, you aren't defeated by it. You're learning from it. Learning from failures and constantly improving products is a key to success in all companies. Listening to customers is a big part of that effort. You have to study what customers say about their problems with your products and be constantly aware of what they want.

But it is surprisingly hard to get bad news from customers passed all the way to the product design groups. Most companies don't have an efficient chain of people and paper between customers and the people who can make major improvements. When the customer data finally reaches the product design group, it often isn't easy for the team to give it the right priority. All of the delays mean that improvements don't happen as fast as they should.

I recommend the following approach to bringing customer complaints and wish lists into the process of product and service development:

1. Concentrate on your most unhappy customers.

2. Use technology to gather rich information on their unhappy experiences with your product and to find out what they want you to put into the product.

3. Use technology to pass the news to the right people in a hurry.

If you do these three things, you'll turn those bad news experiences into an exciting process of improving your product or service. Unhappy customers are always a concern. They're also your greatest opportunity. Listening and learning rather than being defensive can make customer complaints your best source of significant quality improvements. Adopting the right technology will give you the power to capture and change complaints into better products and services fast.

For example, *any* employee of Promus Hotels, based in Memphis, Tennessee, can give customers their money back if they are not satisfied. A no-questions-asked money-back guarantee from a service company like Promus means something. The company has a good reason to fix the problem right away. And because every employee can act on the guarantee, employees watch for quality. So how does Promus stop customers using the guarantee for a free stay and complaining when nothing was really wrong? Technology. All complaints are dealt with by the same main computer. It can quickly identify anyone who goes from hotel to hotel claiming poor service and getting money back. Promus then sends a nice letter, regretting that the hotels could not meet the customer's standards and inviting him to stay in a competitor's hotels.

◆

If your customers can contact you electronically with their problems, you need to be prepared to answer quickly. When a customer mails a letter to a company, he or she doesn't expect a reply for a week, but the customer knows that the e-mail arrives in a few minutes, if not seconds. It's usual for businesses to respond to e-mail within a few hours or overnight. A few days is "slow." If you take weeks to reply, customers will take their business elsewhere. Because e-mail is so much easier to send than paper mail, you're likely to get many more responses, too. So when you ask for electronic responses, make sure you have the staff and the internal systems in place to handle them quickly.

Listen to your customers and take their bad news as an opportunity to turn your failures into the improvements they want. Companies that invest early in digital nervous systems to capture, analyze, and build on customer opinion will stand out from the competition. You should examine customer complaints more often than company finances. And your digital systems should help you change bad news into improved products and services.

Know your numbers

Jiffy Lube was the world's number one servicer of cars, but it was unprofitable when the Pennzoil Company bought it in 1991. By 1997 Jiffy Lube earned $25 million, the highest earnings in its history and an increase of 14 percent over 1996 earnings. Jiffy Lube serviced 21 million cars, an increase of 1.2 million over 1996. Driving this new success was a daily flow of information from each store to headquarters and back. Customer service information from all 1,600 Jiffy Lube outlets is sent to headquarters at Houston every night. Headquarters does immediate analysis on the figures. Beginning as early as 5 A.M., up-to-date data is available to each Jiffy Lube outlet. For example, if people in one neighborhood are not using their Jiffy Lube outlet as much as expected the manager of that outlet will know about it.

"Know your numbers" is a basic business principle. You need to gather your business's data at every step of the way and in every interaction with your customers—and with your partners, too. Then you need to understand what the data means. The numbers shouldn't be your only concern but you should objectively understand everything possible about your business. If you're considering exchanging short-term profits for long-term gains, for example, you need to know as closely as possible the cost of that trade. Companies can use the data they collect to improve the efficiency of their businesses, strengthen their relationships with both customers and partners, extend their businesses in new ways, and develop better service and new products.

There are two ways to use customer data. The first is to gather the numbers that show trends and patterns on which to base analysis, planning, and decisions. The second is to collect detailed information on the individual customer so that you can provide personal service. By creating a digital flow of information from start to finish, businesses are able to create tight links between knowledge management, commerce, and business operations. At Microsoft we showed big improvements as soon as we started using MOET (Microsoft Order Entry Tool) to take customer orders, and MOET is now an advanced website for electronic commerce worldwide.

To use information well, you need to capture it digitally from the start and analyze it in digital form at every stage of your business processes. "Every stage" includes not just what happens within your company walls, but also what happens with both your customers and your suppliers. Knowing your numbers can produce big changes in all of your business relationships and give you a significant competitive advantage.

The business side of any company starts and ends with deep analysis of its numbers. Whatever else you do, if you don't understand what's happening in your business factually, and you're making decisions based on soft data or emotion, you'll eventually pay a big price. Numbers give you the factual basis for the directions in which you take your products. They tell you objectively what customers like and don't like. They help you identify your highest priorities so that you can take fast action. Nothing else can take the place of understanding your numbers at a working level. Sometimes my friend Steve Ballmer, Microsoft's president, surprises the members of a product group by knowing their pricing structures and sales numbers—and the competitors'— better than the people presenting a plan to him. He has a way of marching into a room and immediately asking the one question the team doesn't have an answer to. He's done the work, and he's thought hard about the issues that come out of the numbers. He sets a high priority on decisions that are based on facts.

The middle managers at a company are the people who should be analyzing the numbers. Other groups can help, but the people who deal with customers and competitive problems need to look at their business in every way possible every day. The analysis should support action and not just more analysis. Analysis should lead you step by step to a decision and to action. You have to think, act, judge, adapt.

Starting with digital numbers doesn't just prevent unnecessary effort and errors. It also sets in motion the best ways to process the data afterward. Being digital from the start drives efficiency in manufacturing, shipping, billing, and other operational processes. Getting the data digitally is also the only way to make sure that you get information quickly enough to respond to customer needs before your competitor does.

This need for good information to drive employees to quick action is one reason that "paper numbers" bother me as much as paper forms do. A printed sales figure or a printed number on customer trends is fixed. You don't have the ability to get in and analyze the detail behind the number, or to e-mail it to somebody to talk about it. With a paper number that looks wrong, you have to get hold of somebody and say, "I'm looking at this report, and this number surprises me." A lot of the time there's an easy explanation: a customer has put in a big order or has canceled one. There's nothing you need to do, but you still want to know quickly why the month's results look strange. If you notice a trend in a paper report, it's hard to send the paper around and get people to analyze it. Over time you stop paying attention because it's so hard to investigate. When figures are in digital form, knowledge workers can study them, attach notes to them, look at them in any amount of detail or in any view they want, and pass them around to get help. A number in digital form is the start of thought and action.

Digital technology also enables a company to create a network of partners that serves its customers better. You can create a virtual company in which everyone is joined together by commerce, knowledge management, and operational systems. Your partners are better connected to you, benefit more from your success, and naturally respond to the same patterns of customer behavior that you do.

When your information systems are designed to create a flow of information to and from your customers, the business processes of the entire supply system will become more efficient. Just-in-time delivery can be a reality for any industry.

Digital information flow makes it possible to create an organization without limits, but it takes a new company culture to turn suppliers from "them" into "us." Traditionally companies have not thought of suppliers as a true part of the overall business process needed to serve customers. Today's approach is that of a "value network," a network of partners enabled by digital information flow. Everyone who touches the product must add value, and communications go forward as well as back. Companies in the value network aren't restricted by heavy chains of process, but can interact and do business with many different sellers as they need to.

◆

If the benefits of knowing your numbers and creating a value network are so persuasive, why don't more companies do it? Why don't more companies create a digital information flow to observe trends? Why don't they follow customer history? The main reason is that too few companies start with digital information. Existing paper systems cause people to assume that data is hard to get and work with. They have to work with piles of papers that they can't organize or analyze. They can't find patterns in their data. They can't turn their paper information into action. Because so few companies are using digital tools internally or with partners today, those firms that act quickly to create a digital nervous system have the opportunity to jump ahead of their competitors.

To make the change to a more efficient virtual company, you need to look first at all of the paper on the desks of knowledge workers and ask: How could digital systems get rid of these piles of papers? As part of this inquiry, think of your business processes as extending far beyond your walls to include the entire network of your partners and customers. You need to develop business processes supported by a fast, reliable flow of information that will enable the customer to drive your responses and the responses of all your sellers as if you were a single unit.

Move people into thinking work

The inevitable result of better computer systems is a smarter use of people's time. With intelligent software continuously searching through its sales data, following trends, and noticing what's selling and what's not, the British chain store Marks & Spencer can use its 500 to 600 buyers much more efficiently.

Instead of working through fat paper reports from the previous day to try to find out whether sales are going well, the buyers can use their time more efficiently, using what the latest data is telling them. If sales are going well, no human action is needed, but the system checks sales data and notices any items whose sales are higher or lower than expected. Reports on these items are created automatically and they are all that buyers must deal with.

Using software to handle routine data tasks gives you the opportunity to provide the human touch where it really matters. There's a dramatic difference between getting a note that was clearly written by a person rather than a computer. It's enormously valuable to have a person working with any customer who is unhappy about something really important, or who has special needs. In a hotel, for instance, smart software can dramatically shorten the check-in and check-out time. Staff can then help customers rather than filling in forms, and guests will enjoy their stays more as a result.

Electronic commerce, though, brings new challenges. In a physical store a sales person can use clues such as the customer's questions, dress style, and body language to assess his or her interests. However, at a Web store no one sees the customer, and the goal is to let the customer do as much shopping as possible for himself or herself. Web store owners then have some interesting information to find out. Based on customer behavior, how do you construct a model of who the shopper is? It requires smart data analysis.

◆

Digital tools for analysis are changing the nature of work. Knowledge workers can concentrate on unusual events rather than on the routine. Of course, people don't like allowing machines to take their decisions for them. But when a database gets big enough and complex enough, the computer can do the initial searching and sorting far better than a human being. We're simply not able to recognize patterns in large amounts of data. And the available data—in databases, file systems, message systems, and websites—is growing all the time. The only way we can get the full value of all this data is to use computer tools to find the useful information.

HarperCollins, the publishing company, uses a PC-based system to follow book sales so that it can print just enough books to meet demand. That way it won't be caught with large stocks of unsold books in stores, which publishers have to take back. After only a year in operation the new system has helped HarperCollins reduce returns of unsold copies of its most popular books from over 30 percent to about 10 percent. Each percentage point represents millions of dollars in savings.

Using software to find useful patterns in large amounts of data is called data mining. It can help to predict whether customers are likely to buy an item because of their age, sex, hometown, and other characteristics. It can also identify customers with similar shopping behavior, and customers with specific tastes, in order to provide improved individual service. An Australian health-care company used data mining to follow buying patterns and discovered a $10 million fraud.

The most common use of data mining is for database marketing, in which companies analyze data to discover customer tastes and then make offers to specific sets of people. For example, American Airlines uses information about the twenty-six million members of its frequent flier program—such as the car rental companies, hotels, and restaurants they use—to develop targeted marketing efforts that have saved more than $100 million in costs.

Data mining is part of customer relationship management (CRM), in which information technology helps companies manage customer relationships individually instead of all together. With the patterns revealed by data mining, you can present your products to a customer in a way that's most likely to increase your value to the customer, and his or her value to you. Cost savings come from having more exact models of customers and so the amount of mailings is reduced. A direct marketing campaign for something like credit cards, for example, would normally get a return of about 2 percent. Mellon Bank USA in 1997 had a target of 200,000 new customers, which would normally mean a mailing to 10 million people. Instead, the bank used data mining to produce models of the most likely new customers. The bank was then able to meet its target of 200,000 new customers with a mailing of 2 million, not 10 million. In addition to reducing costs, each new customer was three times more profitable than usual because data mining had targeted the customers whose needs best matched Mellon Bank's services.

This personalization will deeply affect all forms of advertising. As digital TV becomes more popular and electronic books become the preferred way to read magazines and newspapers, almost all advertising will move away from mass advertising to personalized advertising. The commercials that appear on screen will differ according to who is looking at them; different neighborhoods or even different homes in the same area could see different commercials. Big companies can become more efficient with their advertising, and small companies can consider TV and magazine advertisements for the first time. Today many types of advertisement are too expensive for any except true mass-market products. Soon even the neighborhood grocer might be able to afford commercials for people living near the store.

Targeted advertisements should make customers happy. They're more likely to see advertisements that are relevant to them. Some people may be worried that advertisers have too much information about them, but software will make it possible for people to reveal only the information they want to reveal. For example, most people wouldn't mind if advertisers were given viewing patterns. Most regular readers of specialized magazines— whether the topic is sports, food, science, gardening, or cars—look at the advertisements as carefully as the articles. If you watch TV in the same way, mainly for one or two interests, you probably wouldn't object to seeing commercials that concentrate on those interests.

Today most data mining systems are quite expensive, ranging from $25,000 to $150,000 for a small or medium-size business to millions of dollars for a big customer like Wal-Mart. One insurance company spent $10 million for a data mining system five years ago. The boss said he knew he could get the same results for a lot less money with today's technology, but the benefits had been worth the investment.

That remark indicates the value of data mining, but these high prices reflect the old days of complex software, in which only the largest organizations, using a lot of staff or hiring specialists, could make good use of data. With the growth of competition in our information-based economy, customer data has become an increasingly important asset. Every company and every knowledge worker must try to get the most out of the company's data assets. These new users can't afford big database budgets or specialized database experts.

Fortunately, as data mining systems become available for PCs, you'll see prices drop dramatically and the use of data mining explode in companies and departments of all sizes. Soon every company will be able to do the kind of analysis that used to be reserved for the richest organizations.

The greatest value of data mining will be to help companies decide the right products to build and the right way to price them. Companies will be able to look at a variety of packaging options and prices to see which are most attractive to customers and profitable to themselves. These possibilities are of special interest to companies that sell information products. Unlike a car or a chair, products such as insurance, financial services, and books cost much more to develop than to produce and have a value fixed more by the customer than by the physical cost of goods. The secret of success with information products is understanding the characteristics and buying habits of your most likely customers.

The power of data mining will help companies to work out how to acquire new customers, whom to market to, how to price their products, and how to attract individual customers. Human creativity and skill are needed to use this information to create new packaging and pricing ideas, to see new products in the patterns of the computer results, and to develop exciting new offers. The better the tool, the more creative they can be.

Managers need to invest in advanced tools that help people work. You should budget 3 to 4 percent of the salary of your knowledge workers to make sure they have the best tools, which free people to use their energy for creative responses to the patterns and trends identified by the computer. Using information to develop new products and services, and to work together more closely with partners and customers, will always remain a uniquely human task.

Raise your corporate IQ

Like reengineering before it, "knowledge management" has been given so many meanings that it sometimes seems to mean whatever someone wants it to mean. News articles on the topic appear regularly. Consulting companies and websites specialize in knowledge management, and a "knowledge management" magazine started in 1998. If reporters talk to a database company, they find that knowledge management is the newest thing in databases. If reporters talk to a network company, they find that knowledge management means the future of networking. But as a general concept—to gather and organize information, pass the information on to the people who need it, and constantly improve the information through analysis and teamwork— knowledge management is useful.

So let's be clear on a couple of things first. Knowledge management, as I use the phrase here, is not a software product or a software category. Knowledge management doesn't even start with technology. It starts with business goals and processes and an understanding of the need to share information. Knowledge management is nothing more than managing information flow, getting the right information to the people who need it so that they can act on it quickly. And knowledge management is a means, not an end.

The aim is to increase corporate IQ. In today's fast-moving markets, a company needs high corporate IQ to succeed. By corporate IQ I don't just mean having a lot of smart people at your company—though it helps to start with smart people.

Corporate IQ is a measure of how easily your company can share information broadly and of how well people within your organization can build on each other's ideas. Corporate IQ involves sharing both history and current knowledge. The workers in a company with a high corporate IQ work together efficiently so that all of the key people on a project are well-informed and full of energy. The final goal is to have a team develop the best ideas from throughout an organization, and then act with the same purpose and concentration that a single, enthusiastic person would bring to a situation. Digital information flow can help groups to function like individuals.

A company's high-level executives need to believe in knowledge sharing, or even a major effort in sharing will fail. Leaders must also show that they themselves are not locked away in a palace, isolated from everyone else, but are willing to engage with employees. Jacques (Jac) Nasser, operations president at Ford, sends an e-mail every Friday afternoon to 89,000 Ford employees all around the world, sharing the week's news—the good and the bad—with everybody. No one checks the e-mail. He talks straight to the employees. He also reads the hundreds of responses he gets each month and assigns a member of his team to reply to any that need an answer.

I don't send out weekly reports, but I do e-mail employees around the world on major topics. Like Jac Nasser, I read all the e-mail that employees send me, and I pass items on to people for action. I find the e-mail that people send me an amazingly good way to stay aware of the attitudes and issues affecting the many people who work at Microsoft.

When business leaders have created an atmosphere that encourages teamwork and knowledge sharing, they need to set up specific knowledge-sharing projects across the organization and make knowledge sharing a key part of the work itself—not an extra that can safely be ignored. Then leaders need to make sure that the people who share knowledge are rewarded. The old saying "Knowledge is power" sometimes makes people keep knowledge to themselves. They believe that this makes them more valuable to the company. Power comes not from knowledge kept, but from knowledge shared. A company's values and reward system should reflect that idea.

Knowledge management can help any business in four major areas: planning, customer service, training, and teamwork on projects. If you haven't done any work on knowledge management in your company yet, consider picking one or two areas in which to begin knowledge management projects. You can use the success of your projects in those areas to encourage knowledge management projects in your other business areas. Within a few years all leading companies will have achieved high levels of digitally aided knowledge sharing.

Knowledge sharing can help brand planning across countries. Coca-Cola set up worldwide communication with its own e-mail system in the 1980s but it saw IT as an expense to be controlled rather than a tool to help better business. When this changed, all systems and functions were made compatible worldwide and the biggest user of technology was marketing, not finance. The marketing tool Inform (Information for Marketing) looks at data about consumer preferences in every country. From sales data, it can tell you what types of people in a small town in South Africa drink Sprite every day and how much they drank last March.

Knowledge management can be used to make response to customers faster. Yamanouchi Pharmaceuticals, at $3.9 billion, is the third largest drugs company in Japan. They and Microsoft have made Web-based information systems an important part of improving quality and speed of answers to customers' technical questions. Product support at Yamanouchi can immediately answer about half the questions that come in from doctors. To find answers to more difficult questions they use Yamanouchi's Web-based PRoduct INformation CEnter Supporting System or

PRINCESS. This uses electronic searches by product and by word. Answers are put into the system for use next time. In 1998, PRINCESS was made available to the sales team. The next step could be to make it available to doctors themselves.

Online training is another area where knowledge management can make things faster and better. USWeb trains people to use technology in business. It has developed SiteCast for interactive seminars. Online training has been really popular at Microsoft. In 1998 twice as many people were training online as in class.

Digital information flow can help in product development, too. Nabisco has some of the most popular foods in the world. About a third of its new products are worldwide successes, a third do OK, and another third underperform. These results are better than average, but with competition increasing Nabisco decided to use information technology more in the product development process. Nabisco didn't need a new product development process. The technology was needed to help the product development team communicate with each other better and faster. A system called Journey now organizes the information that used to be anywhere on any desk in the office. All of the people involved in the development of any new product need only to click on the product to find all the information about it. For example, Nabisco developed a new product and something in the product was changed. The people writing the description of the product on the label saw the change online and changed the label immediately.

Knowledge management is a fancy term for a simple idea. You're managing data, documents, and people's efforts. Your aim should be to improve the way people work together, share ideas, sometimes argue, and build on one another's ideas—and then act together for a common purpose. The boss's role in raising a company's corporate IQ is to create an atmosphere that promotes knowledge sharing and teamwork, to make a priority of those areas in which knowledge sharing is most valuable, to provide the digital tools that make knowledge sharing possible, and to reward people for contributing to a full flow of information.

Big wins require big risks

To be a market leader, you have to have big goals. You can't just look at the past or the current state of the market. You also have to look at where it's likely to go, and where it might go under certain circumstances, and then direct your company according to your best predictions. To win big, sometimes you have to take big risks. Big bets mean big failures as well as successes. Today, looking back, it's easy to believe that Microsoft's current success was inevitable. But at the time we made our big bets—including starting the company as the first personal computer software firm—most people thought we would fail.

Many leading companies hesitated to move to new technologies for fear of ruining the success of their existing technologies. They learned a hard lesson. If you don't take risks early, you'll decline in the market later. If you bet big, though, only a few of these risks have to succeed to provide for your future. Microsoft's current goals include improving the PC's performance beyond all existing systems, developing computers that "see, listen, and learn," and creating software to power the new personal companion computers. These plans are Microsoft's response to the future, in which all machines will use digital technology and need to work with one another. Whether or not these plans succeed, one fact is clear: we have to take these risks in order to have a long-term future.

Risk taking is natural in a new industry. The computer industry is about as far into its development as cars were in the 1910s and planes were in the 1930s. Those industries went through revolutionary, and often messy, technical and business change before they became stable, and the same thing is happening in the computer industry.

Develop processes that give people power

A business has processes that are similar to the basic biological processes that keep us alive. One of these processes is the function that defines the company's reason for existing—its manufacturing process, for example. This function has to be as efficient and reliable as the beating of a heart.

A second kind of automatic process in business is administrative—the process of receiving payments, paying bills and salaries, for example. The administrative processes are as essential to a business as breathing. If the basic operational processes of your business fail, your company fails.

Because the basic operational processes are so important—and so expensive—most big companies began to invest heavily in automating them years ago. But too often the automated processes were isolated from one another. Overall efficiency wasn't nearly as good as it could be. Until recently, for example, in the manufacture of some aircraft parts only 10 percent of the original metal was actually used in an aircraft. The manufacturing process had been improved at many individual stages along the way rather than as a whole. There was an enormous amount of waste.

I have talked about business operations such as financial and other administrative systems in other sections. In this section I concentrate on production processes. An automated production process is necessary, but not enough on its own to make a company competitive today. A good digital nervous system can help you develop your employees into knowledge workers, changing your company's basic production processes into a competitive advantage.

First, you need to use information technology to understand the inner workings of the process itself better in order to make it both more efficient and more responsive to changing circumstances. Entergy Corporation of New Orleans has increased the efficiency of its power plants with a new process-control system. This allows plant operators to adjust plant efficiency and analyze performance trends as they occur. Operators can actually look inside the plant systems in order to understand exactly how the machines are functioning and to work out whether a minor change or a repair might save an expensive repair later.

An intelligent PC-based system makes sure that the highest-priority items are repaired first. The process-control system actually shows operators the cost of reduced efficiency if the temperature is ten degrees lower than it should be, for example. By attaching a dollar figure to operational decisions, Entergy is turning its operators into business people, giving them the information they need to run their units efficiently, and making them a lot more responsible for their decisions. And because production costs for Entergy's plants are available to senior staff electronically on a minute-by-minute basis, the company can improve its profits by moving power production constantly to those units that are delivering the most cost-efficient energy.

Then you need to be able to get data from your production process to inform other business systems. The Stepan Company, which produces cleaning chemicals, has developed a process-control system that has raised the plant's output by 300 percent and saved the company millions of dollars through more efficient use of its equipment. But the efficiency gains are not as valuable to Stepan as the way that its process-control system can deal with changing customer demands.

Finally, and most important, you need to feed the data from your production process to your production workers so that they can improve the quality of the product itself. If you provide the right technology to help production workers do fast analysis, they'll turn data into information that will help you improve design and reduce faults. Developing a digital nervous system allows you to give more power to as many of your workers as possible.

In the new organization the worker is no longer a part of a machine but is an intelligent part of the overall process. Some metal workers now have to know mathematics to work out angles from computerized designs. Water-treatment companies train production-line workers how to do computerized measurement and math. New digital copiers require the service personnel to have an understanding of computers and the Internet, not just skill with a screwdriver.

Human beings remain essential in operational processes that have to constantly improve and adapt to changing circumstances. An efficient production line needs people—well-informed, responsible people. As we organize tasks into processes, we give workers more responsibility. Computers will take over some jobs, but they will mean that many other jobs are no longer boring.

When people can concentrate on whole processes, their work is more interesting and challenging. Simple tasks will disappear, or be automated or built into a bigger process. Work that involves repeating the same task over and over again is exactly what computers and other machines are best at—and what human workers are poorly suited to and almost always hate. Managing a process instead of performing a task makes someone a knowledge worker, and good digital information flow enables knowledge workers to play their unique roles.

Most companies have been willing to give information tools to their high-paid office staff whose job is information work. Entergy and Stepan are proving that building systems around information flow and giving information tools to line workers can also provide enormous value. Entergy is changing all of its key business processes and pushing information and decision-making down to the operational level. Stepan is using information to manage its plants as a whole to adapt to changing customer needs. Both of these companies are applying knowledge management to business operations to analyze and improve production, quality, and failure rates. Digital tools bring more intelligence to their business operations.

Give your workers better jobs with better tools, and you'll discover that your employees will become more responsible and bring more intelligence to their work. In the digital age you need to make knowledge workers out of every employee that you can.

Chapter 4   Special Projects

No health-care system is an island

A few years ago, a new Microsoft employee was called back to his home state because his mother had suffered a mild stroke. When she was well enough to leave the hospital, Mrs. Jones (not her real name) stayed with her sister while her son completed plans to move her near him. Mrs. Jones largely recovered but was never able to live on her own again, and her periods of good health were interrupted by hospital stays to treat more and more serious problems.

The medical events of the last two years of Mrs. Jones's life show the best and the worst of the American health-care system. She received good care, including a number of very new treatments, from three different hospitals and more than a dozen doctors in two different states. As her physical abilities declined, her middle-class family was able to find good facilities providing greater degrees of care. Medicare and her own private insurance paid most of the bills; she and her family paid the rest. Her many doctors, nurses, and other care givers were professional and kind.

But the system was far from perfect. When Mrs. Jones left the first hospital for her sister's hometown fifty kilometers away, a communication failure between doctors meant that her medicine was kept at full strength when Mrs. Jones should have been on a declining dose. By the time she arrived in the North West, side effects of the high dose meant that she had to go into hospital immediately. Because her records didn't come with her, a number of expensive tests had to be repeated.

The same thing happened when she changed hospitals a year later. Her final three-week hospital stay, which did not involve any surgery, still cost $25,000. At one point, a doctor confused her with another patient and told her next doctor that her recent hospital stays were "an abuse of the system." This was less than a week before Mrs. Jones died.

These and other problems went on even though Mrs. Jones had her family to help her work through the confusing medical and social services options. Her son and daughter-in-law took turns spending many hours standing in line at one agency or on the phone with another. And it took a year before they could persuade one hospital to stop billing them for services that had been paid for in full.

Because of the many hospitals, doctors, care facilities, and public and private agencies involved, the amount of paperwork was enormous. Consider the number of people this paperwork represented. For every doctor and nurse who treated Mrs. Jones, there must have been a dozen billing people in several different organizations. It was like an old-fashioned military operation. For every soldier in the field, you had twenty people behind the lines handling administration.

Most experts estimate that 20 to 30 percent of the annual trillion-dollar cost of the US health-care system is spent on paperwork. In hospitals that number could be as high as 40 to 50 percent. A single week's stay can create as many as a hundred pieces of paper. And, making things worse, about 13 percent of the one to two billion claims each year in the United States are returned for errors.

Paperwork and complexity have risen even as the US health-care industry has shifted to "managed care" in an effort to reduce costs, prevent fraud, and provide appropriate care. With managed care, an organization will contract with a group of doctors to provide medical services toward managed results, and for fixed fees. More than 160 million people in the United States were in managed-care plans at the beginning of 1997, the last year for which figures are available.

Doctors understand the need to control costs but feel buried in rules and layers of management. They're afraid that their medical options may be limited and that the care of patients may suffer. They have also made the situation more complicated by treating patient files as business records and often hesitating to share them with competing doctors. And they've largely been opposed to computers, although that's mainly because early medical systems were clumsy and expensive. Oddly, the managed care that many doctors love to hate may become the primary force that extends information systems into patient care and returns control of patient care to doctors. When you put enough clinically helpful information in front of doctors, they see the benefits and ask for more.

Patients, meanwhile, are recognizing how much more information is available to them on the Web and how this information gives them a sense of control and responsibility in maintaining their own health.

Clinical benefits have also encouraged health-care bosses to push for better information systems. Until now, health care has applied only 2 to 3 percent of its earnings to information technology, compared with the banking industry's 15 percent. Although health care is a high-technology field, the technology has been applied to individual treatment systems, not to information flow. Often the information software that is used is not designed to work with other information software, despite all the health-care areas that should share data: the laboratory, the blood bank, charting, billing systems, and the machines that watch over patients.

Organizations have had to build special interfaces between the different software programs. A typical health-care organization can have hundreds of these interfaces. One organization currently manages 1,800 different interfaces. This complexity is one reason it has typically taken two years for a health-care organization to buy a new system and another two years to install it—too slow by any standard.

Today the situation is more encouraging. The US government has passed laws that require a standard to be defined for electronic finance and administrative dealings, including computer-based patient records. Better information handling in medical organizations will be a requirement in the future. Some health organizations, recognizing that their patients' needs can't wait, are showing strong leadership. They're proving that a digital nervous system can be enormously valuable in all areas of patient care: from emergency services through hospital treatment, keeping in touch with patients, and long-term trend analysis.

◆

Imagine you had a health-care system in your local community built from digital parts. An intelligent emergency system gets you to the hospital quickly, and all the important information on your medical history and current medical condition feeds immediately into the hospital's computers. A doctor uses a touch screen, keyboard, or pen to order your treatment. Digital instructions are sent off to the laboratories. Computers supply laboratory results electronically. These and other reports are online for easy review by any doctor, on site or off. The system will tell doctors about any possible problems with the treatment or differences from the approved clinical path. Billing is handled automatically. Systems that process computer deals uncover fraud or unusual use.

Instead of spending half their time on paperwork, doctors and nurses spend almost all their time treating you and their other patients. Test results and bills reach you in simple, understandable language. All the information about your treatment and medicine is assessed automatically over the longer term to help prevent problems.

Your care after hospital is also scheduled automatically. You find medical information on the Internet and so your meetings with health workers are more informed, whether you communicate with them over the Internet, by e-mail, or you meet in person. You use e-mail to ask routine questions of your doctor and to be reminded about continuing health programs.

When you change health plans, all your medical history goes with you instead of being lost or following after you several months later. Doctors use your history to identify trends in blood pressure, weight, and other patterns that might reveal a serious developing problem. Systematic medical analysis of the whole community makes the authorities aware of any worrying public health trends much sooner and more accurately than has been possible before.

If health-care communities take an approach based on PC and Web technologies, abilities like these do not have to cost a fortune. PCs enable a step-by-step approach using standardized software. PCs are also now being used to control specialized machines such as blood and tissue analyzers, reducing their costs and enabling their data to be shared.

PCs are powerful enough to handle hundreds of thousands of claims or inquiries per hour. All together, the technologies described in this chapter would cost less than $5 million for a typical health-care organization. This is not a small amount of money, but it is minor compared with the amount most health organizations spend on paper-based work and stand-alone computer systems today. With paperwork making up 20 to 30 percent of the $1 trillion-plus per year earnings of the US health-care system, the current cost is $200 billion to $300 billion annually—more than the entire earnings of many countries.

Today the lack of information systems in doctors' offices is the biggest barrier to improving patient care. Only about 5 percent of offices in the United States use computer systems in their clinical work. Computerizing a doctor's office will cost from $10,000 to $50,000 for each one, but doctors can quickly recover the costs. A five-doctor office in Hammond, Louisiana, invested about $50,000 in PC patient systems that made it easy for doctors to enter data; the office saved $60,000 the first year in typing costs alone.

It will take a big effort from health-care providers to improve health care through digital information. The technology is available today. An investment in a shared infrastructure and tools will enable not just a huge reduction in costs, but better health treatment for everyone. Change will be driven by two groups: patients who insist on being better informed and more involved in their own health, and health professionals who use these new tools to provide better care. Together they'll use a digital nervous system to turn the islands of health care into a single continent.

Take government to the people

Government, maybe more than any other organization, can benefit from the efficiency and improved service that flow from digital processes. Developed nations will lead the way in creating paperless processes to reduce administration. Developing nations will be able to provide new services without ever having to deal with clumsy paper methods.

But most governments are far behind business in using the tools of the digital age. Businesses going digital are stuck with many paper forms because governments are not yet online. The reason for this delay is a lack of organizational purpose. Because government processes use a lot of paper and people, in the past making them more "efficient" often meant a reduction in service. It's common for governments to forbid agencies to close any offices, which simply forces them to struggle to do more with less.

At the same time, there are few pressures to provide better service. Citizens can't take their business to another tax agency or vehicle-license office. Government agencies tend to concentrate on their own internal organizational needs rather than the broad needs of citizens and businesses. As an example, consider the paperwork involved in hiring a child-care provider in the United States. The employer has to know that there are five agencies involved, each with its own set of forms. This complication, rather than a desire to avoid paying the taxes, explains why so few people follow the rules. In this and many other cases, to the average citizen government remains a threatening knot of separate agencies and rules.

But digital processes and the Web lifestyle give government the opportunity to change so that it is organized around citizens rather than administration. Governments can take five major steps to help make the digital age a reality in their countries. The first two involve improving government services; the last three involve creating an infrastructure so that a country's businesses can compete in the digital age:

1. Put government employees on e-mail and get rid of paper filing. Make sure that all information inside government is digital.

2. Put government services online with an interface designed for the user. Publish everything on the Internet.

3. Attract investment by technology companies and encourage electronic commerce, sometimes with financial help, but more often with joint projects. Create a standard for the electronic identification of businesses and citizens.

4. Remove the rules that stop the communications industry from working efficiently. Encourage major investments in the communications infrastructure.

5. Improve the skills of citizens by using technology as part of education and training systems at all levels.

Government, like businesses, can make better use of software tools and e-mail to get far more benefits from technology investments. In developed nations many government employees and public officials already have PCs on their desks, and developing nations can put in a PC infrastructure for a small cost. The use of e-mail alone promotes cooperation between agencies and enables public officials to respond better to inquiries. Some US politicians are beginning to use e-mail to stay in touch with citizens, and Australia's national parliament is using digital work flow to make sure that inquiries are followed up.

Governments need to make the decision to use digital information flow instead of paper. Internet publishing should be standard. Printed documents should be rare. The savings would be immense. The US government alone spends one billion dollars annually printing documents that are already available on the Web. Most copies of these documents are for public officials whose offices are already online. Most of the printed copies end up in the trash in the nation's capital. Web publishing of all government documents can reduce costs and make information far easier to find. Digital systems are also better for complex documents. The government description of a transport plane, which companies need if they want to bid to build it, weighs more than a house in printed form, but the data would easily fit on a couple of CDs.

◆

An online approach does more than simply reduce paper expenses. Web technology makes it possible for governments to provide a single point of contact for the public, a single online "face" to structure information according to what is important to the citizen.

In several Swedish cities, for example, webpages organize a variety of services from various levels of government. Citizens can quickly find passport offices, tax authorities, and national insurance offices. They can get reports from public meetings and other public documents. They can even get real-time reports on public transport, based on electronic information from the vehicles, either using the Internet or kiosks. A kiosk is just a PC designed for public use.

As the Internet provides the best way to interact with government, all citizens need to use it, even if they don't have PCs themselves. If electronic kiosks that work like bank cash machines are placed in post offices, libraries, schools, and other public buildings, they can help governments improve services while reducing the cost of delivery.

Online systems are most useful for citizens and most efficient for government when they have more than one purpose. Governments should review all their dealings with citizens that require them to stand in line or fill out forms. Government should bring together all the agencies involved to develop a single system for handling all contact with citizens.

The Irish government, using An Post, the Irish postal service, has done this best. An Post kiosks process bill payments, issue passports, issue licenses for vehicles, pay benefits, offer savings and investment plans—even sell stamps. Each kiosk is a tiny city hall, covering the work of half a dozen agencies. With many of the 1,000 An Post sites in small towns with fewer than 2,000 residents, the kiosks serve 1.26 million people each week—half the Irish population—and handle more than $9 billion each year. Changing or adding new operations is very easy.

For government dealings like these, as well as for all commercial deals, security is essential. Security has two elements: protection of personal data while it's moving over the network and identifying the person carrying out the operation. Today there is encryption technology that is strong enough to protect the security of any electronic movement on a network, but US export controls on encryption technology restrict US firms from building it into their products. Since this does not keep encryption technology out of the hands of criminals, the software industry is working to change the US government's mind on this issue. In practice, the encryption that can be used is strong enough that in most cases the security of data in a network is not the weak link. Electronic data is as safe as data in other forms.

Identifying the user is equally important. You don't want someone else getting into your government records or your bank account. Smart cards are a solution to identity problems, as with the cards for bank cash machines. In Spain a new kiosk system will let anyone find out general information about social benefits by going through a touch-screen menu, but the person needs a smart card to find any personal information.

Though such cards are just like the bank cards used around the world, some people are worried that the government might collect too much information about citizens. Some nations have privacy laws that prevent a single card or database from containing all information about a citizen, so in some nations there will be two cards: one for financial operations with business or government and another for health care.

Widely available information and the ability to put a lot of information on smart cards will cause societies to look again at the question of how information can be used. Should any employer be able to see a job candidate's police record? Or just organizations such as schools, which hire people who work closely with children? In the end these are political questions rather than technological issues. Each country will have to decide on the kinds of personal information that will be allowed on smart cards. Even if their use is restricted to identity only, the efficiency gains and the prevention of fraud are worth the investment. In London, 200 trial kiosks of a system like An Post's reduced benefit payment fraud by £750,000 in the first year. When installed at all 1,500 post offices, the kiosks are expected to save £150 million per year.

◆

Less developed countries may assume that a digital approach to government is out of reach, but countries without systems can start fresh with new technology, which will be less expensive than manual approaches. Developed countries have older systems that often must be joined together.

Examples from around the world make it clear that many of the advances are happening in smaller governments—smaller nations and cities, counties and provinces, and the state levels of larger nations. Smaller governments are less complex and they can experiment and work out solutions on a smaller scale. For larger governments, the lesson is to start with smaller projects to develop the necessary skills and see how citizens respond. Concentrate at first on projects that directly touch citizens and particularly ones that get rid of organizational complications for the public.

King County in my home state of Washington is probably ahead of many governments in the amount of information it publishes online, but the county does not yet package information or operations simply. To get a building permit in rural King County, you must obtain information from many sources: the phone book, phone calls to the county office, two or three printed documents, and the department's website. A single well-structured website, with all the information and links involving all steps in the building permit process, would remove most of the complications, and could automate some of the steps.

Savings from new digital systems would represent a significant portion of every government's budget. The US military recently found that it was spending more money to process and approve travel permits, $2.3 billion, than it was spending on travel itself, $2 billion. The US government budget is $27 billion for food stamps, $25 billion for social benefits, and $13 billion for public housing. These programs all have enormously expensive paper-based administrative systems that eat up 30 percent of the money. Good digital systems could push this below 10 percent.

Citizens are becoming more aware of the power of the Web and they are no longer willing to accept the idea that government service should be slow or confusing. No customer would stand in line for two hours to get service from a private business. Why should a worker stand in line for two hours at a government office and lose two hours of pay, when by using the Internet he could get his license or pay his fees and be at work on time?

Government alone, by building key services around the Internet, will provide a big reason for citizens to move to a Web lifestyle. If the government, usually the largest "business" in any country, is a leader in the use of technology, it will automatically lift the country's technical skills and drive the move to an information market. Building an information economy will make all the companies in the country more competitive. The Information Age benefits from having more people involved. As more and more countries join in, the importance increases for all countries. World trade will be done digitally.

No government can put a fully digital approach in place immediately, but every government can begin now with strong first steps that benefit citizens and make them feel that the government is working for them. The main principle should be that citizens should never again have to fill out lots of forms or go to lots of places to get information.

As one government official said in conversation about his new website, which lets people download a hundred years of county records online, "People can tell when you're trying to help. They know the difference between a government agency trying to help them and one that's just getting in the way."

Create connected learning communities

PCs can give more power to teachers and students than any other group of knowledge workers. Students are pure "knowledge workers," since learning is all about acquiring knowledge. Teachers will be able to use the Internet to share with each other and to allow students to explore a subject in new ways. With a solid infrastructure in place, some schools are already benefiting from PCs in the classroom. Many schools struggle to find the resources for these new tools, but clever programs have shown that there are rewards for the effort.

The success of PCs as educational tools requires teacher involvement. Without teacher training and making PCs central to the teaching program, they will not have a big effect. Many PCs have gone into computer "laboratories" where they sit, seldom used. Schools need to shift from treating the PC as a subject—teaching about technology—to including it in all areas of the teaching program: teaching with technology. More and more schools are now showing that PCs used as learning tools can have a strong influence.

In the Western Heights Independent School District, just west of Oklahoma City, Oklahoma, teachers were enthusiastic when the district provided training the summer before it introduced

PCs. More than 200 of its 230 teachers signed up. Most teachers have a great love of learning and they'll get excited about anything that will help kids learn. What teachers don't want is to be thrown into something they have not had the opportunity to learn about and become comfortable with.

Western Heights is a small, seven-school district with a moderate industrial tax base. The student population contains a mix of cultures. About 65 percent of the kids qualify for free or reduced-cost school lunches because they come from homes with lower incomes. This is not the school district that you might expect to lead the advance into the Information Age. But in the past three years the district has voted three times to spend a total of more than $6.8 million in local funds to create maybe the leading technology-based teaching program in the country. The community sees the investment as the only way to break the cycle of poverty that could trap these children if they go unprepared into the digital world.

A PC can be a powerful new teaching tool for teachers. They find they can make kids more interested in lessons by including photos, films, and links to Internet pages. One teacher at Western Heights starts his class each day with fresh news from the Internet. PCs are part of each teacher's life in class at Western Heights. Teachers also use e-mail to communicate with one another about common issues. They don't have to wait for the district meetings that occur a couple of times a year. They can reach out to fellow teachers with questions and get answers back quickly.

"People may not realize how alone teachers are in the classroom," Joe Kitchens of the Schools Department at Western Heights says. "Most teachers remain behind closed doors all day. They have little time for sharing experiences or interacting with other teachers. There are only a few times a year when they can gather together. E-mail stops them being isolated." Kitchens also jokes that teachers are able to complain to him more than before. They expect him to answer their questions immediately over e-mail.

An important way to take advantage of investing in technology is to use the school infrastructure to benefit the entire community. Basic computer skills are one type of education that can be applied in any job. In most countries, one out of every ten information technology (IT) jobs is not filled. The United States and Europe each need more than half a million new trained IT professionals in the next several years. Rapidly developing areas such as India and Latin America may have greater shortages.

Highdown School in Reading, England, is paying for the infrastructure it needs through a mix of private and public money. Highdown School expects the community to contribute. Adults can get online technical training either at the Reading schools, which open on evenings and weekends for that purpose, or at home. Fees for this service go toward maintaining and expanding the IT system.

Most knowledge workers in the United States have their own PC, but even at the best of schools there are usually more than seven students for every PC. It's expensive for schools to buy PCs for every student, especially when PCs become out-of-date every three years or so. For this reason there's a fear that the gap between the "haves"—those families that can afford PCs at home—and the "have-nots"—those that cannot afford PCs at home—will create a major gap in opportunities. Creative approaches in providing PCs to every student are beginning to help solve this problem.

One project started in the early 1990s in Melbourne, Australia, where Bruce Dixon, a teacher interested in technology, saw significant differences in teaching results when he could use half a dozen computers for his classes instead of just one. He realized that, for the best results, students had to use PCs as a tool for all their work—in all their classes and at home as well as at school.

Out of many meetings came the idea of having all the students finance their own machines. Dixon, by then a technology advisor, worked out a financial plan. For a monthly fee, students get a machine and software. The seller provides service, and when the student graduates the family keeps the machine. It's still difficult for all families to afford the fees. Families that are wealthier can afford the typical forty-dollar monthly fee over a three-year period. Many families can afford to pay a small amount. Business and community organizations can make up the difference. Whatever the amount, the family contribution is basic to this program, as it gives the students and their parents a sense of owning and being responsible for the computer and for its role in the students' education.

Programs like this have spread to schools all over the world. The effects have been impressive. A recent report shows that students who regularly use computers gain many skills. They write more often and better; they have better analysis skills; they express themselves more creatively; they work more independently, and they are better at problem solving and critical thinking.

◆

One of the most forward-looking ideas is to use PCs to offer a variety of ways to learn. About fifty different major theories attempt to describe individual learning styles. Most of the theories identify similar qualities. In the simplest terms, some people learn better by reading, some by listening, some by watching someone else do a task, some by doing the task. Most of us learn by a mix of all of these methods. And all people have different levels of ability and different personalities and life experiences that affect how well they learn. New software is helping students learn, whatever their learning style or ability. Software can present information in many different forms that can be adapted to the individual student much more easily than paper methods.

PCs can help change the learning experience from the traditional approach—a teacher talking at the front of a classroom, with reading tasks—to a more hands-on approach that takes advantage of the natural curiosity of students of all ages. PCs enable students to explore information at their own speed, to learn from sound and pictures as well as from text, to do experiments, and to work together with other students.

PCs are the primary tools for working and communicating in the digital age. The PC and the Internet change one thing completely: they provide every student in every school and community with information and ways of working that, before now, were not available even to students at the best schools. Educators will take advantage of that to help their communities. PCs are a new teaching and learning tool, and educators who use them will be the agents of change.

Chapter 5   Expect the Unexpected

Prepare for the digital future

Customers are the main people who benefit from the increased efficiency of information technology, and the benefits will increase as the economy becomes more digital. The other people who benefit are business people who take advantage of digital methods faster than their competitors. The solutions I have talked about in this book are the result of the vision and leadership of business people who used IT to serve their customers better.

Business leaders who succeed will take advantage of a new way of doing business, a way based on the increasing speed of information. The new way is not to apply technology for its own sake, but to use it to change how companies act. To get the full benefit of technology, business leaders will make their processes and their organizations simpler and more modern. The goal is to make business responses nearly immediate, and to make strategic thought a process that goes on all the time—not something that's done every twelve to eighteen months, separate from the daily flow of business.

New technology should provide better information to every worker who might possibly use it. Knowledge workers are the brains of the company. If they're disconnected from the company's important data, how can they work, how can they take responsibility? You can give people tasks and authority, but without information they can't do anything. Knowledge is the best power tool. If important information about production systems, product problems, customer crises and opportunities, lost sales, and other important business news gets through the organization in minutes instead of days, and if the right people can be working on the issues within hours instead of days, a business obtains a huge advantage. This change in the structure of processes is more important than any other change since mass production.

Every company can choose whether to lead or follow the digital trends. The Internet is changing the basis of industries in real time. Winning is not easy. Digital information flow and giving power to employees is part of achieving and maintaining competitive advantage. A belief in giving people power is the key to getting the most out of a digital nervous system. Knowledge workers and business managers benefit from more and better information, not just senior management. When employees get a couple of good tools that deliver better results, they demand more. It's a positive cycle.

However you organize your company, one thing is clear: it is impossible to manage a company totally from the center. It is impossible for a single person or group of people to stay on top of every issue in every area of a business. Leaders need to provide planning and direction and to give employees tools that enable them to gather information and understanding from around the world. Companies that try to direct every action from the center will simply not be able to move fast enough to cope with the speed of the new economy.

In business the argument between central authority and the individual is the difference between the old-style way of thinking, which saw workers as lazy people who needed to be controlled, and the theory that workers are creative and should be given responsibility. Digital processes support the idea that workers can—and will—do more if allowed, enabled, and encouraged to think and act.

This argument about the center and the individual is not just academic. The choice affects the design of companies and systems. The design of the first manned space ship shocked the original pilots years ago. There were no manual flight controls. Don't worry, said the scientists. The system would fly the ship. The pilots, like the monkeys before them, were just there for the ride. The pilots resisted. They all had experience of "advanced" systems that failed when things got difficult. The pilots won, and on several flights the pilots' skill brought them home safely when the central, programmed system failed. The issue is not whether computers can fly better than pilots. Today planes and space ships use large amounts of computer technology to extend the human ability to fly. The issue is whether someone "at the center," away from the real circumstances, can possibly predict all of the things that can change or go wrong—whether in space or in a business office.

Many parts of business can be improved through digital systems, but it will take a number of years to improve every single part. Every bit of data in a company should be in digital form, and easy to find, including every file, every record, every piece of e-mail, every webpage. Every internal process should be digital and connected to every other process. Every operation with partners and customers should be digital. You should allow partners and customers to have all the data that is appropriate to them, and they should do the same for you.

Human beings are not the biggest animals, the strongest or fastest, or the sharpest in sight or smell. We survived and grew successful because of our brains. We learned how to use tools, to build shelter, to invent agriculture, to keep farm animals, to develop civilization and culture, to cure and prevent disease. Our tools and technologies have helped us to shape the environment around us.

I'm a positive person. I believe in progress. I'd much rather be alive today than at any time in history—and not just because in an earlier age my skills wouldn't have been as valuable and I'd have been a good candidate for an animal's dinner. The tools of the Industrial Age extended the capacities of our muscles. The tools of the digital age extend the capacities of our minds. I'm even happier for my children, who will grow up in this new world.

By joining the digital age enthusiastically, we can accelerate the positive effects and do better with the challenges, such as privacy and the problem of "haves" and "have-nots." If we sit back and wait for the digital age to come to us on terms defined by others, we won't be able to do either. The Web lifestyle can increase the involvement of citizens in government. Many of the decisions that need to be made are political and social, not technical. These include how we make sure that everyone can get on the Web and how we protect children. Citizens in every culture must join in the discussion about the effects of digital technology, to make sure that the new digital age reflects the society they want to create.

The digital world certainly makes it tough and uncertain for business, but we will all benefit. We're going to get improved products and services, better responses to complaints, lower costs, and more choices. We're going to get better government and social services that cost a lot less. This world is coming. A big part of it comes through businesses using a digital nervous system to improve their processes. A digital nervous system can help business define itself and its role in the future, but success or failure depends on business leaders. Only you can prepare your organization and invest in ways that take advantage of the rapidly dawning digital age.

Digital tools extend the abilities that make us unique in the world: the ability to think, the ability to express our thoughts, the ability to work together to act on those thoughts. I strongly believe that if companies give their employees the power to solve problems, and give them powerful tools to do this with, they will always be amazed at how much creative and independent thinking will appear.

ACTIVITIES

Chapter 1

Before you read

1 Read the Introduction to the book. These dates are all important. What happened in each of these years?

1955   1973   1975   1980   1981   1985   1995 (2 events)
1999   2005

2 Look at the Word List at the back of the book. Find new words in your dictionary. Then answer these questions.

   a If you download software from the Internet, where does it go?

   b If you automate production processes, do you need more or fewer factory workers?

   c If you take part in an online seminar, do you use your computer or your phone?

   d In this book Bill Gates discusses "digital nervous systems." What kind of technology do you think the systems use?

   e Why do companies organize marketing campaigns?

   f The Internet is a communications infrastructure. What does that mean?

3 The title of this chapter is "Information Flow is Your Lifeblood." Discuss the different ways that people, companies, and countries can benefit from more and faster information.

While you read

4 Write the endings to these sentences, as they appear in the text.

   a Information work is ....

   b Manage with the force of ....

   c Nobody can help you if your processes aren't ....

   d No company can assume that its position in the market is ....
      ....

   e Information technology gives you the data that leads to ....
      ....

   f It takes brains to understand the physics of a rocket; it takes a computer to ....

   g To do information work, people in the company have to be able to ....

h Companies that are struggling with too many unproductive meetings don't lack ....

i A digital nervous system seeks to create company excellence out of individual excellence to ....

j Your managers should have information of the same quality that ....

k Today we have all the pieces in place to achieve ....
....

l A good network, a good e-mail system, and easy-to-build webpages are everything you need for ....
....

After you read

5 Bill Gates writes, "The best way to put distance between your company and the crowd is to do an excellent job with information." With another student, discuss why this is true, and how it can be done.

Chapter 2, pages 20–32

Before you read

6 In what ways has the Internet changed the way that companies work over the past few years? What changes do you imagine will happen in the future?

While you read

7 Are these sentences right (✓) or wrong (✗)? At the time when this book was written, according to Bill Gates,

a the United States had the world's highest percentage
of people with home PCs. .....

b notebook computers were changing into computer
notebooks. .....

c the change to the Web lifestyle would happen in the
next five years. .....

d all companies needed to use the Internet to talk to their
customers. .....

e travel agents would have to change their way of doing
business. .....

f Barnes & Noble only sold books online. .....

g Merrill Lynch lost a lot of business when it developed an online service. .....

After you read

8 Bill Gates refers to "Adam Smith's ideal market."

    a What is this ideal market?

    b What do you know about Adam Smith? When did he live? What was the name of his most important book? What did he write about? What were his new ideas, and how do you think the Web can help to make them work? Use the Internet or a library to find out information that you don't know.

9 Work in a small group. Act out the conversation with the German bankers. Ask and answer questions, and try to come to an agreement about your vision of the future.

Chapter 2, pages 32–45

Before you read

10 In the early twentieth century, electricity brought changes to people's lives. In the late twentieth century, the Internet also introduced great changes. Which of these inventions do you think has made the greater difference? Which has been of most benefit?

While you read

11 Match the names with the information about them, at the time of this book.

    a Autoweb.com .....

    b Chrysler .....

    c Dell .....

    d Marriott International .....

    e NASA .....

    f The US Commerce Department .....

    g The city of Amsterdam .....

    1) The role of its online sales team changed to consultancy as the website developed.

    2) It wanted its customers to be able to pay bills online.

3) Online sales were expected to increase greatly in the near future.

4) Its websites allowed people to discuss local issues online.

5) Its website allowed customers to find exactly what they, personally, wanted.

6) It responded to complaints about its dealers.

7) Many people visited its website because they wanted more news than they could get from newspapers and television.

After you read

12 What are the advantages and disadvantages of physical stores and online stores? Do you think that online stores will completely replace physical stores in the future? Discuss your ideas with another student.

Chapter 2, pages 45–55

Before you read

13 In your experience, how is the world of banking changing in response to new technology?

While you read

14 Find the correct endings, below, to these sentences. According to Bill Gates,

  a companies would have fewer …   .....

  b medium-size and small companies would be able to …   .....

  c there would be new opportunities for individuals to …   .....

  d companies that gave more freedom to their employees would be able to …   .....

  e computer chips would have …   .....

  f Banco Bradesco would collect …   .....

  g Compaq would have data on …   .....

  1) more and more transistors.

  2) more information about its customers.

  3) full-time employees.

  4) create teams quickly for large projects.

  5) sales per day.

  6) work independently.

  7) hire the best people.

After you read

15 Think about a factory in the middle of the twentieth century and one today. How have work practices changed, and how have computers and the Internet helped to make these changes?

16 Do you think it is better for people to have a full-time job with one company, or to work on short projects for a number of companies? What types of people might be best suited to each type of work? Discuss this with another student.

Chapter 3, pages 55–66

Before you read

17 Imagine that you are the CEO of a large company. You are going to give a talk to your employees with the title, *Bad news must travel fast*. What will you say to them?

While you read

18 Complete each sentence.

    a A manager should want to hear bad news because..................

    ....

    b In 1995 Microsoft was caught by surprise by ....

    ....

    c Gates predicted that three years after he wrote this book, every product that Microsoft made would be.....................................

    ....

    d The Promus Hotels' money-back guarantee helped the company because ....

    e Customers who send you e-mails expect ....

    f A "value network" is ....

After you read

19 Answer these questions.

    a What was the problem with Windows 95?

    b What happened to Internet use in 1993?

    c What helps to get more work done before meetings?

    d Which people in a company should analyze the numbers?

    e What must everyone who touches a product do?

20 Bill Gates says, "A number in digital form is the start of thought and action." With another student, discuss how a number on a piece of paper is less useful.

Chapter 3, pages 66–79

Before you read

21 Which of these two predictions for the future do you think will happen? Give reasons for your answer. Which one do you think Bill Gates believed in?

    a Almost all work will be done by machines, controlled by a few people. Most people will be unemployed.

    b Computers and the Internet will allow people to do more interesting work. Boring jobs will disappear.

While you read

22 Underline the wrong word in each sentence and write the right word. At the time of writing,

    a Marks & Spencer had 500 to 600 stores.   ....

    b HarperCollins tried to sell the exact number of books that its customers wanted.   ....

    c American Airlines collected information on its frequent buyers.   ....

    d Mellon Bank used data finding to reduce their mailings.   ....

    e Nabisco decided to use new technology in the product development process.   ....

    f The Stepan Company had improved its response to changing government demands.   ....

After you read

23 In this book, Bill Gates writes about a digital nervous system, which is in some ways similar to the human nervous system. In what ways can computer think better than human beings? In what ways can we think better?

24 Roleplay this situation with another student.

    Student A: You are the CEO of a company. Your working systems are very old-fashioned and paper-based and you are losing customers. You are worried, but you are also afraid that new systems will mean that you lose control.

    Student B: You are a Microsoft employee. You can see how digital technology will improve the company's performance and you understand the CEO's fears. Try to persuade Student A to accept the changes.

Chapter 4

Before you read

25 How efficiently do medical services work in your area? What problems are there?

While you read

26 Choose the best ending for each sentence. At the time of writing,

    a the American health-care system's main problem was
        1) bad care.   **2)** bad communication.   **3)** high cost.

    b most doctors resisted
        1) the use of computers.   **2)** paperwork.   **3)** higher costs.

    c most governments had too many
        1) software programs.   **2)** services.   **3)** paper forms.

    d you could get a passport from a kiosk in
        1) Sweden.   **2)** Ireland.   **3)** Spain.

    e users of data could be identified by
        1) encryption.   **2)** hardware.   **3)** smart cards.

    f schools needed to stop treating the PC as
        1) a separate subject.   **2)** a learning tool.
        3) a teaching program.

After you read

27 Answer the questions.

    a Mistakes could have been avoided in Mrs. Jones's case. Can you give two examples?

b What reasons does Bill Gates give for doctors' unwillingness to use computers?

c Why have governments been slow to use computers?

d Bill Gates lists five steps the government can take to help make the digital age a reality. What step do you think will be the easiest? Which will be the most difficult? Why?

28 Discuss which uses of computers in government, schools, and hospitals mentioned by Bill Gates would be most useful where you live.

Chapter 5

Before you read

29 In the future, do you think everyone will be involved in the Web lifestyle, or will more and more people turn away from it and look for a simpler way of life, without computers?

While you read

30 Put these statements in the order that the information is given.

a All data in a company should be in digital form.

b Knowledge workers must be connected to the company's data.

c Information technology helps customers.

d The digital world will improve products, services, and government.

e You can't manage a company totally from the center.

f The Web lifestyle can give people more political power.

g Successful companies must use information technology.

h Information must move through a company quickly.

After you read

31 In Chapter 5, Bill Gates summarizes his argument. Note down his main points, then compare your list with another student's. Are your lists the same?

Writing

32 Write about your company or a business you know well. How close is the company to achieving the "paperless office"? Do you agree that the paperless office is an ideal solution?

33 Write "A Day in the Life" of a family who have adopted the Web lifestyle twenty years from now.

34 List ways in which a digital nervous system can help banking and financial firms. Use the German bank referred to by Gates, Merrill Lynch, and Banco Bradesco as examples.

35 Moore's Law says that the power of processors doubles every eighteen to twenty-four months. Imagine what processors will be capable of doing ten years from now. Describe a home of the future.

36 Write a letter from Promus Hotels to a customer who has used the system to get their money back three times by claiming poor service.

37 Imagine that you work for Microsoft. An old-fashioned company has asked you to look at the way it works and write a report on how this could be improved. Write the report.

38 The government in your country wants to improve the health service and has money to do so. Some people want to spend this on more doctors and nurses; others feel that better computers and information systems would be more effective. Write your ideas.

39 Your local council wants to use the Internet to include citizens more in decisions. They have asked you to write about how this could be done. Write your report.

40 Do you think that changes in the way business works will make life better for people in all parts of the world or only for people in more advanced countries? Write your ideas.

41 Write a letter to a friend. Tell them about this book, whether it has changed your ideas, and why you think they should read it.

Business Word List

bankrupt	in a state of financial ruin
board	a group of people who manage, advise or watch over a company
bond	a contract document promising to repay money borrowed by a company, often with **interest**
capital	money and property used to start a business or to produce more wealth
commerce	the activities involved in buying and selling things
corporate	relating to a large company, or **corporation**
currency	money, in coins and notes, which is used in a particular country
equity	the value of a property or of a company's shares; **equities** are shares that give you some of the profits
interest	payment received by a lender for the use of their money, or paid by a borrower
merge	to join together into one company
negotiate	to try to come to an agreement with another person through discussion
objective	a business aim
option	a contract giving a right to buy or sell at a particular price in a certain period
retail	the sale of goods to customers
return	the profit or income from an investment
security	something that you promise to give someone if you cannot repay money borrowed from them; *securities* are investments in stocks and shares
share	one of the equal parts into which ownership of a corporation is divided
speculate	to take a business risk in the hope of a gain
stock	investments in a company, represented by **shares** or fixed-**interest securities**
underwrite	to accept financial responsibility for something

WORD LIST

3-D (three-dimensional) (adj) having, or seeming to have, length, depth, and height

automate (v) to do a job using computers and machines instead of people

bandwidth (n) the amount of information that can be carried through a computer connection or telephone wire at one time

boundary (n) the line that marks the edge of something; the limit of what is possible

campaign (n) a series of actions that are intended to achieve a particular result; a **marketing campaign** aims to persuade people to buy a product or service

chip (n) a small piece of material, with electronic parts on it, used to hold memory and for processing in computers

click (on) (v) to press a button to make a computer do something

compatible (adj) able to be used together without problems

consumer (n) someone who buys or uses goods or services

digital (adj) using a method of storing, processing, and communicating information in which the information is represented by numbers

download (v) to move information or programs from a computer network to your computer

downsize (v) to reduce the number of people who work for a company, to reduce costs

encryption (n) a change in the form of data in order to keep that information private

function (n/v) the usual purpose of something, or the activities expected of a person; if something *functions* in a particular way, it performs in that way

hardware (n) computer machinery and equipment

IQ (n) the level of someone's intelligence

infrastructure (n) the basic systems that an organization or a country needs to work in the right way

interact (v) to communicate with other people and work with them

interface (n) the way you put information into a computer program; the way two things affect each other

online (adj/adv) connected to other computers through the Internet, or available through the Internet

outlet (n) a place of business from which goods are sold; a store

outsource (v) to use workers from outside a company; to buy supplies from another company instead of producing them yourself

plant (n) a factory and all its equipment

processor (n) the control unit of a computer that is the central exchange for all information inside the computer

satellite (n) a machine that has been sent into space and goes around the Earth to send and receive electronic information

seminar (n) a short course or a special meeting that people attend to learn about a particular subject

software (n) the sets of programs that tell a computer how to do a particular job

strategy (n) a planned series of actions for achieving something

transistor (n) a piece of electronic equipment that controls the flow of electricity in machines like televisions, computers

virtual (adj) made, done, or seen on the Internet, not in the real world; being a representation, not something real

The Story of the Internet
Stephen Bryant

The Internet is the fastest growing phenomenon in technology
the world has ever seen, revolutionising business and the lives of
almost every person on the planet – in less than ten years.

The Double Helix
James D. Watson

James D. Watson and Francis Crick won the Nobel Prize in 1962
for the discovery of the double helix, the structure of DNA. In this
book, James D. Watson tells the exciting story of this discovery.

Brave New World
Aldous Huxley

Aldous Huxley's *Brave New World* is one of the great works of
science fiction. It is the year After Ford 632 in the New World.
People are born and live by scientific methods. There is worldwide
happiness and order. Then John comes from the Savage
Reservation to the New World and with him he brings strong
emotions – love, hate, anger, fear. Suddenly, danger threatens the
New World.

*There are hundreds of Penguin Readers to choose from – world classics,
film adaptations, modern-day crime and adventure, short stories,
biographies, American classics, non-fiction, plays ...*

For a complete list of all Penguin Readers titles, please contact your local
Pearson Longman office or visit our website.

www.penguinreaders.com